YO-CRX-848

DATE DUE

DEMCO 38-297

264515

TO MY MOTHER

MUSICOLOGICAL STUDIES & DOCUMENTS

THE ORIGIN OF THE TOCCATA
BY
MURRAY C. BRADSHAW

AMERICAN INSTITUTE OF MUSICOLOGY
ARMEN CARAPETYAN, Ph. D.
DIRECTOR

MUSICOLOGICAL STUDIES & DOCUMENTS

28

THE ORIGIN OF THE TOCCATA

MURRAY C. BRADSHAW

AMERICAN INSTITUTE OF MUSICOLOGY
1972

© 1972 BY ARMEN CARAPETYAN

PREFACE

The subject of the toccata began to attract the serious attention of musicologists in the early decades of this century. In 1925/26 Leo Schrade published an article, "Ein Beitrag zur Geschichte der Tokkata," in which he discussed such important features of early toccatas as their function, style, and significance. A few years later, Erich Valentin wrote the first and only monograph on the subject, a survey which followed the development of the genre from its origins through Bach's death in 1750. Otto Gombosi, in an essay of 1934 titled "Zur Vorgeschichte der Tokkata," proved that the term "toccata" cannot be limited merely to keyboard pieces. These three writings make up the essential bibliography of the toccata, and even if several later contributions are considered — such as Suzanne Clercx's "La toccata, principe du style symphonique," Hans Hering's "Das Tokkatische," and Valentin's concise introduction to *Die Tokkata*, the seventeenth volume of *Das Musikwerk* — the number of scholarly efforts devoted to this significant genre remains quite slim.[1]

The time seems right, then, both for a new approach to the toccata and for a revaluation of some of the more commonly accepted ideas on the genre. The first chapter of this study is devoted to the different sorts of compositions "toccata" referred to in the Renaissance age, and specifically, since the focal point of this volume is the keyboard toccata of the Venetian school, to some of the more important and universally accepted notions about these pieces.

---

[1] Leo Schrade, "Ein Beitrag zur Geschichte der Tokkata," *Zeitschrift für Musikwissenschaft* VIII (1925-1926), 610-635; Erich Valentin, *Die Entwicklung der Tokkata im 17. und 18. Jahrhundert (bis J. S. Bach)* (Münster i. Westf., 1930); Otto Gombosi, "Zur Vorgeschichte der Tokkata," *Acta Musicologica*, VI/2 (1934), 49-53; Suzanne Clercx, "La toccata, principe du style symphonique," *La musique instrumentale de la Renaissance* (Paris, 1955), 313-326; Hans Hering, "Das Tokkatische," *Die Musikforschung*, VII/3 (1954), 277-294; Erich Valentin, *Die Tokkata* ("Das Musikwerk," XVII; Cologne, 1958).

In the second chapter, the origin of the keyboard works is taken up, and new conclusions about their structure are reached. The final chapters trace this structure in pre- and post-Venetian compositions up to the toccatas of Bach.

I wish to thank especially Professor Edward E. Lowinsky of the University of Chicago for his constant encouragement and advice in the writing of this book. Without his detailed criticisms this work and many of the ideas it contains would have been inconceivable. I am also indebted to Professor Gilbert Reaney and Dr. Armen Carapetyan for kindly reading through my typescript and making many valuable suggestions, to Professor Robert Tusler who in numerous conversations helped to enlarge the scope of this study, and finally to Professors Thomas Marrocco and Paul Sellin who helped with many of the difficult translations.

Murray C. Bradshaw
University of California at Los Angeles

CONTENTS

PREFACE 7
LIST OF MUSICAL EXAMPLES 11

Chapter I. Toccata: Definitions and Assumptions . . . 13
Chapter II. The Origin of the Venetian Keyboard Toccata 19
Chapter III. The Keyboard Prelude and Lute Toccata of
           the Renaissance 49
Chapter IV. Toccata and Prelude in the Seventeenth Century 67

APPENDIX OF MUSIC

Introduction 87

Intonationi di Gio. Gabrieli

1. Primo Tono 93
2. Secondo Tono 93
3. Terzo & Quarto Tono 94
4. Quinto Tono 94
5. Sesto Tono 95
6. Settimo Tono 95
7. Ottauo Tono 96
8. Nono Tono 96
9. Decimo Tono 97
10. Vndecimo Tono 97
11. Duodecimo Tono 98

Intonationi di Andrea Gabrieli

12. Primo Tono 98
13. Secondo Tono 99
14. Terzo Tono 100
15. Quarto Tono 102
16. Quinto Tono 103

17. Sesto Tono	105
18. Settimo Tono	106
19. Ottauo Tono	108
20. Toccata di Andrea Gabrieli. Del Quinto Tono	109
21. Toccata di Andrea Gabrieli. Del Sesto Tono	111
22. Toccata di Andrea Gabrieli. Del Ottauo Tono	117
23. Toccata di Andrea Gabrieli. Del Nono Tono	122
BIBLIOGRAPHY	131
INDEX	137

LIST OF MUSICAL EXAMPLES

1. Venegas de Henestrosa, *Fabordón llano*, psalm tone V (*Libro de cifra nueva*, 1557) 19
2. Venegas de Henestrosa, *Fabordón glosado*, psalm tone V (*Libro de cifra nueva*, 1557) 20
3. Cabezón, *Fabordón glosado*, psalm tone V (*Obras de música*, 1578) 21
4. Andrea Gabrieli, *Intonatio*, tone V (*Intonationi*, 1593) 22
5. Giovanni Gabrieli, *Intonatio*, tone X (*Intonationi*, 1593) 27
6. Andrea Gabrieli, *Toccata*, tone V (*Intonationi*, 1593) 28
7. Opening of the imitative section of Andrea Gabrieli's *Toccata*, tone VI; Gregorian psalm tone VI 31
8. Girolamo Diruta, *Toccata*, tone I (*Il Transilvano*, 1593).......... 31
9. Claudio Merulo, *Toccata*, tone V (*Toccate*, 1604) 34
10. Ruggiero Giovanelli, *Falsobordone*, tone I (*Regole, Passaggi di Musica*, 1594) 38
11. Leonhard Kleber, *Finale in re seu preambalon* (*Tabulatur für die Orgel*, 1524) 51
12. Leonhard Kleber, *Preambalon in La* (*Tabulatur für die Orgel*, 1524) .. 53
13. Hans Kotter, *Anabole in fa* (Organ Tablature, c. 1520) 55
14. *Preambulum in Fa* (Regensburg FK 21) 56
15. William Byrd, *Praeludium*, tone VIII (Fitzwilliam Virginal Book) ... 57
16. Joanambrosio Dalza, *Tastar de corde*, tone II (*Intabulatura de Lauto*, 1508) 60
17. P. P. Borrono, *Thochata*, tone IV (Giovanni Antonio Casteliono, *Intabolatura de leuto*, 1536)............................ 61
18. Francisco Guerrero, *Falsobordone* for lute and voice, tone IV (Miguel de Fuenllana, *Orphenica lyra*, 1554)............... 62
19. Francisco Guerrero, *Falsobordone* for lute and voice, tone V (Miguel de Fuenllana, *Orphenica lyra*, 1554)............... 63
20. Sweelinck, *Toccata*, tone I 67
21. Scheidt, *Toccata*, tone II 69
22. Anonymous, *Präambulum*, tone II (Lüneburger Orgeltabulatur KN 208[1]) 71
23. Hans Leo Hassler, *Toccata*, tone II 73
24. Samuel Mareschal, *Quinti toni, transpositus* 76
25. Johann Jacob Froberger, *Toccata*, tone V 79

CHAPTER I

TOCCATA: DEFINITIONS AND ASSUMPTIONS

The constant evolution of musical forms, even within a single period of time, brings with it a continuous change in the meaning of terms used for the various genres and forms of music. During the Renaissance, for instance, the term "toccata" referred originally to brass fanfares played at ceremonies and festive occasions, a type of toccata Suzanne Clercx has traced far beyond the confines of the Renaissance, finding evidence of it, for instance, in Monteverdi's "toccata" or overture to *Orfeo* (1607), the sonatas of Mauritio Cazzati (d. 1677), the *sinfonie* or opera overtures of 17th and 18th century Italy, and, finally, the symphonies of the classical period[1].

But in the course of the 16th century it was also employed for some lute compositions. In 1508, Joanambrosio Dalza prefaced five pieces with the words "*tastar* de corde" ("sounding" or "playing strings") — apparently a predecessor of the term "toccata" — and almost thirty years later, Giovanni Antonio Casteliono's *Intabolatura de leuto* (1536) included four "tochate," two of which were to be played "nel fine del Ballo."[2]

Finally toward the end of the century, musicians used it to describe certain keyboard compositions. Yet even among these keyboard works the term referred to several different kinds of music. The "toccata ligature e durezze" is characterized, as the title indicates, by syncopation and dissonance and by a strongly chromatic style in slow tempo with occasional points of imitation. The "toccata in modo di trombetto" is simply a fanfare transferred to the keyboard.

---

[1] *La musique instrumentale de la Renaissance*, 313-326; Gombosi, in *Acta Musicologica*, VI/II (1934), 52, noted that "fanfare" toccatas appeared as early as 1393.
[2] For the titles and contents of these two collections see Howard Mayer Brown, *Instrumental Music Printed Before 1600* (Cambridge, 1965), 1508² and 1536⁹.

But the toccata proper — without any additional or supplementary title, except perhaps one that indicates the mode or tone — denotes the most well-known type of keyboard composition in which sustained chords and brilliant scale passages alternate with imitative sections. This became the classical keyboard toccata, one that exercised a powerful influence on the development of Western keyboard music. Furthermore, the term toccata is most often associated with this particular sort of composition. The present study raises anew the origin of this form and style.

The first printed toccatas of this kind — that is, with sustained chords, brilliant scale passages, and imitative sections — appeared in 1591 in an edition by Sperindio Bertoldo. This initial stage of the genre ends in 1604 with two volumes, the first containing three works by Annibale Padovano (d. 1575) and five by anonymous composers, the other of ten by Claudio Merulo. Thirteen pieces by various composers are included in Diruta's *Il Transilvano* (1593), and in the same year Gardano brought out four toccatas by Andrea Gabrieli. Claudio Merulo's first volume appeared in 1598. If Merulo's nine and Giovanni Gabrieli's ten works in the National Library of Turin are considered, the repertoire consists of more than sixty compositions.[3]

Although the printed editions cover a mere thirteen years, several generations of composers are involved. Andrea Gabrieli (b. ca. 1510) is the oldest, Girolamo Diruta (b. 1561) the youngest. Annibale Padovano, Vincenzo Bell'Haver, Sperindio Bertoldo, and

---

[3] For the titles of these six collections see Claudio Sartori, *Bibliografia della musica strumentale italiana stampata in Italia fino al 1700* (Florence, 1952), 1591c, 1593b, 1593c, 1598b, 1604d, and 1604e, as well as Brown, *Instrumental Music Printed Before 1600*, 1591⁴, 1593³, 1593⁴, and 1598⁹. The manuscript with additional toccatas by Merulo and Giovanni Gabrieli is the second volume of the Renzo Giordano collection in the Turin library. Although it contains several more toccatas, I have confined myself to those works that were originally printed as well as to the total output of Merulo and Giovanni, since these last are available in modern editions. This furnishes a repertoire of 64 compositions, more than enough to afford a representative picture of the genre. Merulo was by far the most productive composer, writing 28 of the 64 compositions. Giovanni Gabrieli is represented by 11, Andrea by 6, Diruta by 4, Annibale by 3, Bertoldo by 2, and Luzzaschi, Romanini, Quagliati, Bell'Haver, and Guami by 1 each. Only five works are anonymous.

Claudio Merulo were born around 1530, Gioseffo Guami around 1540, Luzzasco Luzzaschi around 1545, Paolo Quagliati about ten years later, and Giovanni Gabrieli in 1557. In addition to Annibale, three other composers — Andrea Gabrieli (d. 1586), Bell'Haver (d. 1587), and Bertoldo (d. ca. 1590) had died before their compositions appeared in print. Except for Bertoldo, Luzzaschi, and Quagliati, all were active, at least for part of their lives, in Venice. In short, keyboard toccatas were being composed before 1575, the year of Annibale's death, at which time some sort of tradition had already been established, and the center of this activity was Venice. A fairly long tradition of playing, of improvisation, obviously preceded the publication of these pieces.

Music historians have made some interesting assumptions about Venetian toccatas. In 1924, Wilhelm Fischer described them as "free" compositions, that is, not based on a *cantus firmus* or any vocal model. They lack, he said, "a vocal standard and, thus, all formal direction; here was the first playground of pure, instrumental music."[4] Ernst Ferand, in 1938, echoed this sentiment when he wrote that these toccatas reveal for the first time a "spontaneous" ("unmittelbar") type of instrumental music, one that acquired its shape directly from the nature of the instrument itself, not indirectly from a vocal model.[5] Quite recently, Willi Apel also grouped the toccata with the "free" forms of 16th century keyboard music, opposing it to liturgical compositions (Masses and so forth), as well as dances, imitative works, and variations. Indeed, he described it as "the second major type of free organ music in the sixteenth century,"[6] the first being the prelude.

Allied to this is another assumption: the toccata has generally been thought to represent an improvisational practice — as one writer put it, "the oldest free and natural form, at least as far as keyboard music is concerned."[7] Gombosi, too, described them as

---

[4] Guido Adler ed., *Handbuch der Musikgeschichte*, I (reprint of the second edition; Tutzing, 1961), 392.
[5] *Die Improvisation in der Musik* (Zürich, 1938), 332.
[6] *Geschichte der Orgel- und Klaviermusik bis 1700* (Kassel, 1967), 215.
[7] Erich Valentin, *Die Entwicklung der Tokkata im 17. und 18. Jahrhundert* (Münster, 1930), 3.

improvisational compositions,[8] and Hans Hering observed that in these pieces "improvisation is raised to a principle."[9] Hence, they were thought to be early examples of keyboard music realized at the spur of the moment — without forethought — even though such "improvisations" were frozen in notation.

A third assumption is that the Venetian toccatas grew out of the keyboard intonation, and that both genres, toccata and intonation, stemmed from the earlier prelude. Valentin, Frotscher, and Ferand, for instance, take this point of view,[10] but Apel, although of the belief that the toccata developed from the intonation, mentions only that intonation and prelude are very similar.[11]

A fourth assumption is that the structural feature basic to the toccata is the contrast between imitative, ricercar-like sections and brilliant virtuoso ones. Fischer, for instance, noted that the toccatas of Claudio Merulo have a ternary structure — "an improvisatory beginning, a ricercar with interludes, and an improvisatory conclusion" — and that these "were the starting point for the further development of the toccata."[12]

A final hypothesis recently put forth by Egon Kenton is that the tonality of these compositions — expressed by such titles as "toccata of the first tone" — is actually quite ambiguous, and that such titles were affixed to these pieces, as he says, purely "for tradition's sake."[13]

One of these assumptions, the relationship of toccata and intonation, is clearly valid, at least from the stylistic point of view. Thirty *intonationi* appeared in Gardano's volume of 1593, the same collection that contained four toccatas by Andrea Gabrieli. These

---

[8] *Acta Musicologica*, VI/2 (1934), 51.

[9] *Die Musikforschung*, VII/3 (1954), 277.

[10] *Die Entwicklung der Tokkata*, 11; *Geschichte des Orgelspiels* (Berlin-Schöneberg, 1935), 82; *Die Improvisation in der Musik*, 70. Hans Heinrich Eggebrecht discusses the different definitions of toccata, intonation, prelude, and other related terms in *Studien zur musikalischen Terminologie* (Wiesbaden, 1955), 905-926 (89-110).

[11] *Geschichte der Orgel- und Klaviermusik*, 212.

[12] *Handbuch der Musikgeschichte*, I, 394.

[13] *Life and Works of Giovanni Gabrieli* ("Musicological Studies and Documents," 16; American Institute of Musicology, 1967), 451.

short compositions "begin with sustained chords, proceed with passage-work in alternating hands, and end with a written-out trill, beginning on the upper note."[14] Although this style was not entirely new, in the hands of Andrea Gabrieli "these elements became much more integrated and are amalgamated into a homogeneous composition consisting of broad, massive chords intertwined with impressively rising or falling scale passages."[15] Brevity in musical thought and unity in style remain the chief differences between the two: the longest intonation consists of only seventeen measures and includes no extended passages in imitation.

Yet, the undeniable relationship between intonation and toccata does not explain the origin of these forms. What gave rise to such a clearly idiomatic style of keyboard writing? Are both forms simply improvisational creations of inspired organists? Why did these compositions find such fertile ground in Venice? It is not enough to consider the Venetian keyboard toccatas a *fait accompli* and to view them chiefly as the cornerstone upon which future composers — Sweelinck, Frescobaldi, Froberger, and Bach, for instance — were to build their more familiar edifices. From all that is known of the practice of composition in the Renaissance, it is difficult to assume that these lengthy pieces, at times so intense in musical expression, were written without composers having some sort of control over them, other than one of a mere contrast of texture. Furthermore, although the Venetians were the first to publish a large group of toccatas, their works gave no hint of expertimentation or insecurity. On the contrary, they were the creations of self-assured musicians who seem to have known exactly what they were doing. The question arises, then, as to whether toccata composers may have had models, perhaps even vocal models, that have so far been overlooked by historians and scholars.

---

[14] Gustave Reese, *Music in the Renaissance* (New York, 1959), 540.
[15] Willi Apel, *Masters of the Keyboard* (Cambridge, 1962), 54.

CHAPTER II

THE ORIGIN OF THE VENETIAN KEYBOARD TOCCATA

About forty years before the publication of the first toccatas, a style quite similar to them occurs in a genre of composition known as the falsobordone (Spanish "fabordón"). In their simplest instrumental form these pieces are exact transcriptions of vocal falsobordoni, compositions that originated in Italy or Spain shortly before 1480 and that became immensely popular in the 16th century. They were most often used in the part singing of Vesper psalms, and the following example of a keyboard "fabordón llano" or "simple falsobordone" might very well have been intended as accompaniment to such a performance:

Ex. 1. Venegas de Henestrosa, *Fabordón llano,* psalm tone V *(Libro de cifra nueva,* 1557), ed. by Higinio Anglés, *MME,* II, 10.

Analysis reveals how close this example is to the Gregorian psalm tone (Ex. 1b), for along with this melody which he placed in the soprano, the composer took over the peculiar form of the psalm tone: two large divisions (measures 1-7 and 8-17) each in turn subdivided into a recitation (1-3 and 8-9) followed by a cadence (asterisks mark the *cantus firmus*, as they will in other examples in this book). In contrast to the two recitations, the two cadences show a slight embellishment of the psalm tone, moderate harmonic change, and a few nonharmonic tones. Except for the initial chord in the first half, the recitation is a homorhythmic repetition of one chord, a device perfectly suitable for the performance of psalm texts irregular in length and accentuation (since these chords would simply be repeated until the cadences of each verse were reached).

Graced with embellishments, such a composition might also have served as an instrumental verset, substituting for the choral psalm verses. A keyboard falsobordone of this very kind does indeed occur in Henestrosa's *Libro de cifra nueva* (1557), the same collection in which the above "simple falsobordone" is found. The style of this "fabordon glosado" or embellished keyboard falsobordone has assumed many characteristics commonly associated with the later intonation: solid block chords, scale passages, sustained beginnings, *a4* texture, as well as brevity:

Ex. 2 Venegas de Henestrosa, *Fabordón glosado,* psalm tone V *(Libro de cifra nueva,* 1557), ed. by Higinio Anglés, *MME* II, 16.

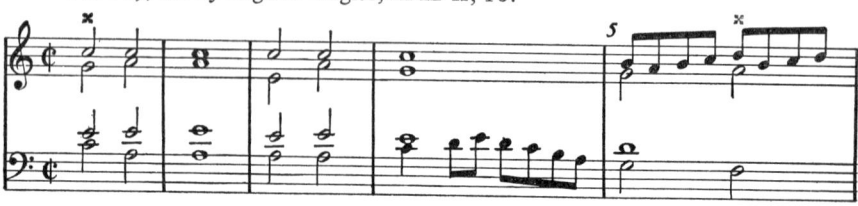

Even though this "fabordón glosado" is a more idiomatic keyboard composition than the first example, it too remains close to the psalm tone form (the two recitations occur in measures 1-4 and 9-10, and the two cadences in 5-8 and 11-18), and the *cantus firmus* of psalm tone V lies in the top part.

But at a very early date the simple psalm tone form was altered, sometimes in rather drastic ways. In several keyboard falsobordoni by Cabezón (d. 1566) as well as in some from Henestrosa's collection, the psalm tone is treated with a new flexibility. In the first place, the musical motion continues right through the middle cadence. Secondly, the simple recitation of homorhythmic chords is abandoned in favor of embellishments during the recitation. Both techniques result in rather important formal changes, since now the larger and smaller two-part divisions of the original Gregorian tone are obscured. One of Cabezón's versets for tone V, transposed down a fifth, illustrates both features.

Ex. 3 Cabezón, *Fabordón glosado,* psalm tone V *(Obras de música,* 1578), ed. by Higinio Anglés, *MME* XXVII (Barcelona, 1966), 61 - 62

There is little to distinguish the two recitations (measures 1-3 and 8-9) from the two cadences, except for the faster harmonic motion of the latter. In measure 9, for instance, the alto motive (see brackets) becomes an integrated part of the following cadence and links the two sections together.

The stylistic similarities between this piece and the earliest intonations are quite remarkable, so much so, that it can confidently be maintained that such falsobordoni served as models for the more assured and brilliant *intonationi* of the two Gabrielis. Andrea's setting of tone V, transposed down a fourth by the composer, affords a convenient comparison:

Ex. 4 Andrea Gabrieli, *Intonatio*, tone V *(Intonationi,* 1593), fol. 15 - 16v

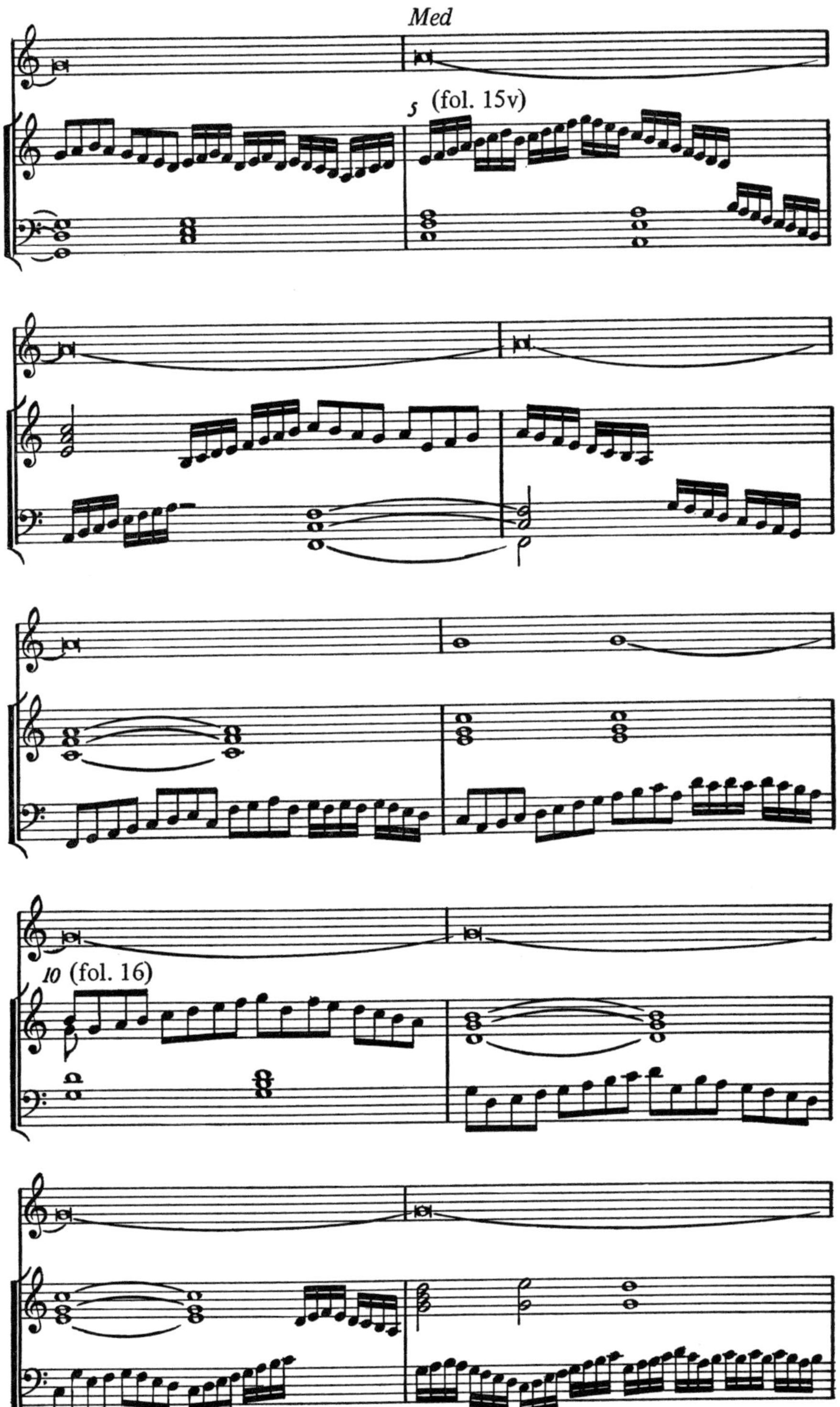
Med
5 (fol. 15v)
10 (fol. 16)

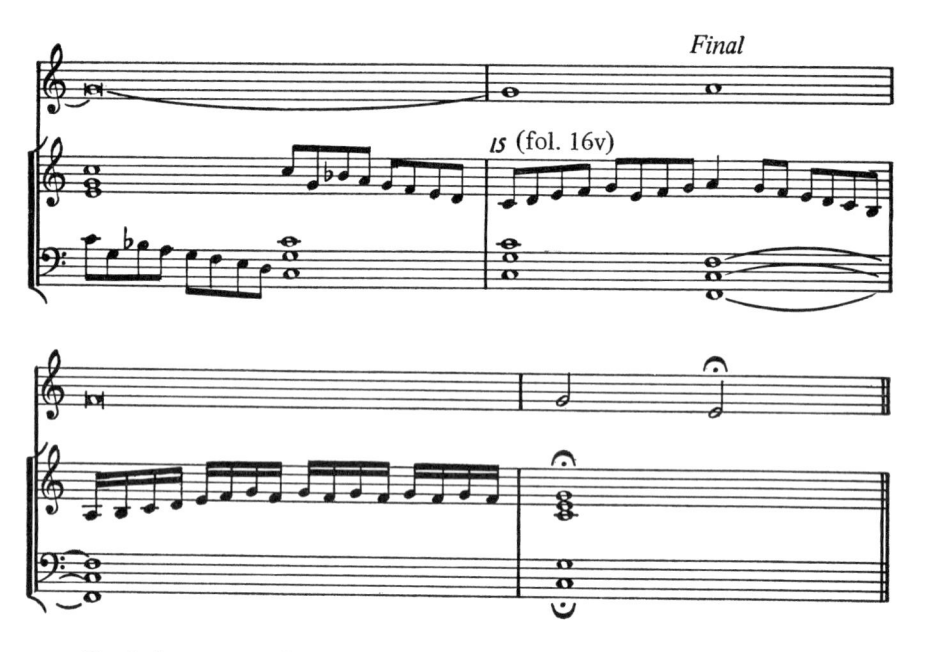

Both have an *a4* texture in which block chords support diatonic scalar embellishments. Both have a continuous structure that is not a result of imitative counterpoint (as in the late 16th-century ricercar) but rather of their own peculiar style and technique. Both have a real bass line that moves essentially by fourths and fifths. Above all, both are founded on a psalm tone.

In order to elucidate this *cantus firmus* procedure, the borrowed psalm tone is placed on a separate staff. Two "cadences" (measures 5-9 and 15-17) follow two "recitations" (1-4 and 9-15). In several intonations the first few chords bear no relation to the opening notes of the Gregorian melody. Nevertheless, every intonation begins and ends on the same harmony, bringing in addition to the *cantus firmus*, another tonal, unifying device to these compositions.

It also points up their function, namely, to supply the pitch for the choir — a function verified by the exact transposition of Giovanni's compositions to different pitches.[1] Furthermore, since

---

[1] Tones I, III (and IV), V, VI, VIII and X are transposed up a fourth, tones VII, IX, and XII down a fifth, tone II up a fifth, and tone XI down a fourth. In Bernhard Schmid's *Tabulaturbuch* (1607), it is noted that Andrea's intonations could be employed "in place of a prelude" ("ane statt [= "anstatt"] der Praeludien"); see the reproduction in Frotscher, *Geschichte des Orgelspiels*, opposite 208.

these pieces are neither versets nor accompaniments but rather preludes with clearly circumscribed functions, the term "falsobordone" would have been out of place. The designation "intonatione," however, suited its purpose admirably. It means simply to play "in the tone" or more precisely "in the psalm tone." The liturgical use of this new term is further corroborated by Francesco Severi in his publication of embellished *vocal* falsobordoni (Rome, 1615). Here, the first verse of every composition, which is always in a simple style, is titled "intonatio," whereas the remaining verses, which are always embellished, are called "falsobordoni."[2]

In some ways, however, Andrea's intonations differ from earlier keyboard falsobordoni. Although the bass line of each usually moves by leaps of fourths and fifths — an essential feature of the choral falsobordone from its beginnings in the late 15th century — Andrea's intonations often approach major and minor tonalities. In the fourth example, for instance, Roman numerals can easily be added to identify the harmonic structure. The composer also emphasized the tonal chords, those built on the first, fourth, and fifth degrees of the scale, rather than the modal third and sixth degrees.

Another difference between the two genres is that Andrea's embellishments cover a wider range, sweeping from the top of the keyboard to the bottom; furthermore, they are no longer restricted to one or two of the parts as in Cabezón's compositions. The rhythmic motion, too, is quicker, more brilliant and driving, and melodic contours have become bolder and more vigorous. This is not empty virtuosity but an entirely new technique of expression, one that heralded the emerging Baroque spirit. It is the difference between Tintoretto's *Last Supper* (1592-94) and *The Holy Family* by Luca Cambiaso (1527-85), between sweeping horizontal lines and nervous energy on the one hand, and rounded forms and tranquil movement on the other.

[2] SALMI PASSAGGIATI PER TVTTE LE VOCI / NELLA MANIERA CHE SI CANTANO IN ROMA / SOPRA I FALSI BORDONI DI TVTTI I TVONI ECCLESIASTICI ... Composti da Francesco Severi Perugino ... In Roma da Nicolo Borboni l'Anno MDCXV ...

A final difference between Andrea's intonations and the earlier works is the "ideal" presence of the *cantus firmus* in the intonations. That is, it is not present in long values, nor is it embellished, nor simply passed from part to part. It is, in fact, not audibly present at all.

The use of such an "ideal" melody was not at all uncommon in the Renaissance. Otto Gombosi, for instance, discussed its presence in ground-bass compositions, in which the familiar bass line *cantus firmus* is only ideally present, and Edward E. Lowinsky has demonstrated similar workings in his article on "English Organ Music of the Renaissance."[3] Hugh M. Miller describes a technique which also makes use of an "ideal" *cantus firmus*.[4] Noting that a collection of twenty keyboard pieces in the British Museum (Additional MS 29996) are headed by the words "all these are upon the faburden of these plainsongs," Miller presents a convincing argument for the following compositional technique: the composer took a plainsong hymn melody, transposed it up a third (or down a sixth), embellished it, and then added one or two voices to this part. Certainly by this time the original Gregorian melody can only be considered "ideally" present. Finally, lest the presence of ideal *cantus firmi* appear incredible to some readers, 20th-century performers of jazz — improvisers just as 16th-century Venetian organists had to be — make constant use of such a technique.[5] The procedure, then, is not restricted to the distant horizons of history.

Such "idealism" of melody had distinct practical advantages, for the composer thought of this borrowed theme less as a concrete melody than as a source for further melodies, harmonies, textures, and formal structures. Andrea Gabrieli, for instance, felt such little restraint in his treatment of the second psalm tone that after presenting the entire melody once he then repeated the last half.

---

[3] See Otto Gombosi, "Zur Frühgeschichte der Folia," *Acta Musicologica*, VIII/III-IV (1936), 121, and Edward E. Lowinsky, "English Organ Music of the Renaissance — I," *The Musical Quarterly*, XXXIX/3 (1953), 386-387, including n. 25 and 26.

[4] Hugh M. Miller, "Sixteenth-Century Faburden Compositions for Keyboard," *The Musical Quarterly*, XXVI/1 (1940), 50-64.

[5] See Frank Tirro, "The Silent Theme Tradition in Jazz," *The Musical Quarterly*, LIII (1967), 313-334.

Even more than Andrea, Giovanni Gabrieli handled the psalm tone in a rather casual fashion, suiting it to his own needs and inspiration. He may employ one-half of it or, as in tone V, present it twice. Bernhard Schmid, who included both Andrea's and Giovanni's intonations in his *Tabulaturbuch* (1607), confused the two composers, attributing Andrea's compositions to Giovanni and *vice versa*. From the point of view of virtuosity, Andrea appears more advanced than Giovanni, but the latter's treatment of the *cantus firmus* is far freer than his uncle's. Giovanni even set tones IX, X, XI, and XII, tones for which no traditional psalm melodies exist. But the composer simply selected some of these familiar tones that were capable of

Ex. 5 Giovanni Gabrieli, *Intonatio,* tone X *(Intonationi,* 1593), fol. 8v

assimilation to the new modes. For example, his intonation for the tenth tone makes skilful use of the first half of tone IV.[6]

If, then, it is concluded that the "free" and "improvisatory" form of the intonation is nothing else than an instrumental elaboration of a psalm tone "ideally" present, what are the implications of this for the keyboard toccata? The larger and more expansive form of the toccata might easily lead to the opinion, exactly because of this seeming freedom, that it is emancipated from a *cantus firmus*. But the astonishing fact is that the toccata too is based on the ideal presence of the psalm tone, and its figurations similarly founded on the simple harmonic progressions underlying the invisible melody. Even though toccatas differ in length and complexity, they are essentially intonations expanded in time by the simple process of repeating the psalm tone, a technique already observed in Giovanni's intonation of the fifth tone. The toccatas, together with Andrea's intonations, represent a distinct technical advance over the earlier falsobordoni but no fundamental change in structure. In the following illustration, taken from the same print of 1593 that contained Andrea's intonations, the psalm tone is again placed over the composition, and Roman numerals indicate the beginning of the *cantus firmus*:

Ex. 6 Andrea Gabrieli, *Toccata,* **tone V** *(Intonationi,* 1593), fol. 21 - 22v

---

[6] For tone IX, Giovanni also used the fourth psalm tone; for tones XI and XII he employed psalm tone V and VIII respectively. Although Andrea's intonations do not go beyond tone VIII, he did write a toccata in tone IX and tone X.

II

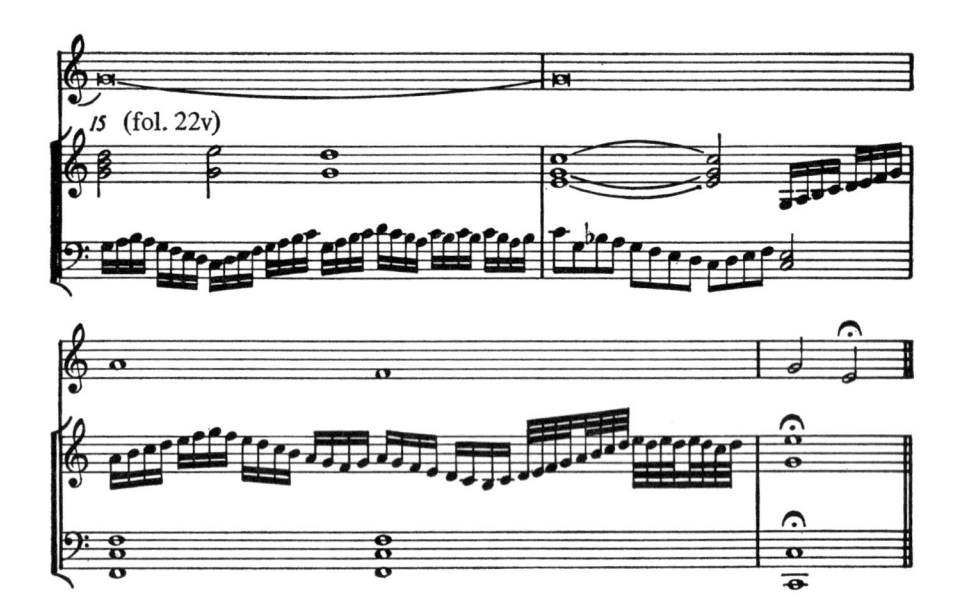

Andrea's second toccata is even more impressive. After *three* presentations of the psalm tone, an extensive imitative section of twenty-seven measures occurs. This, in turn, is followed by a last presentation of the borrowed melody, in which both the final cadence and its last few notes are repeated several times. Yet the melody remains an ideal one, and the resulting work — as all Venetian toccatas — is a musical parable or allegory in which structure is determined by considerations external to the work itself. To speak of repetition in a toccata, therefore, is not strictly correct. What Andrea does is to employ and reemploy the psalm tune, not audible as such, as a scaffold for everchanging ideas. He writes variations, as it were, without incorporating the theme in any material fashion, and thus repeats it only by implication.

This composition illustrates another cardinal feature of Venetian toccatas, one taken over from the intonation and certain keyboard falsobordoni, and that is a continuous, on-flowing structure: the music never comes to a complete stop until the very end. Another characteristic, and one quite often employed by other Venetian composers, is the derivation of the subject for the fugal section from the plainsong melody (in this case the final cadence; see Ex. 7 where the chant is also given):

Ex. 7 Opening of the imitative section of Andrea Gabrieli's *Toccata,* tone VI (*Intonationi,* 1593); Gregorian psalm tone VI.

In many of these compositions it is quite easy to trace the psalm tone. With Andrea's pieces this process is facilitated by slow-moving harmonies and a simple texture. Even Diruta, the youngest composer of the group, employed this straightforward technique in one of his toccatas. He, too, presented the psalm tone only once, but reversed the two sections, beginning with the last half and ending with the first:

Ex. 8 Girolamo Diruta, *Toccata,* tone I^a *(Il Transilvano,* 1593*),*
ed. by Carl Krebs, "Girolamo Diruta's Transilvano," *Vierteljahrsschift für Musikwissenschaft,* VIII (1892), 383

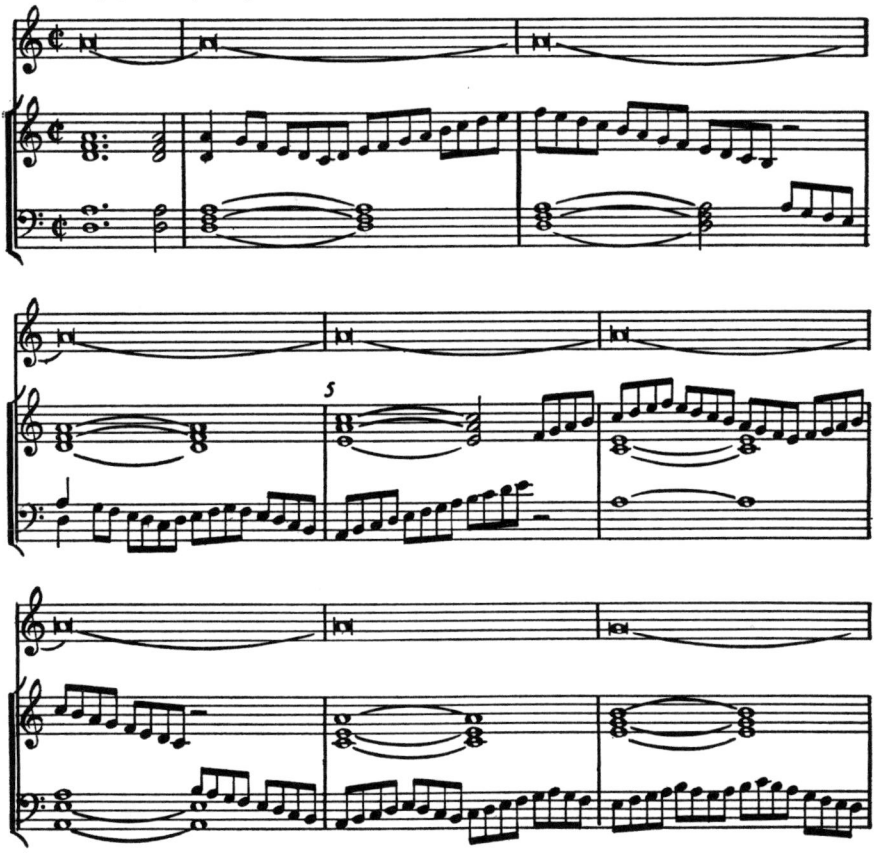

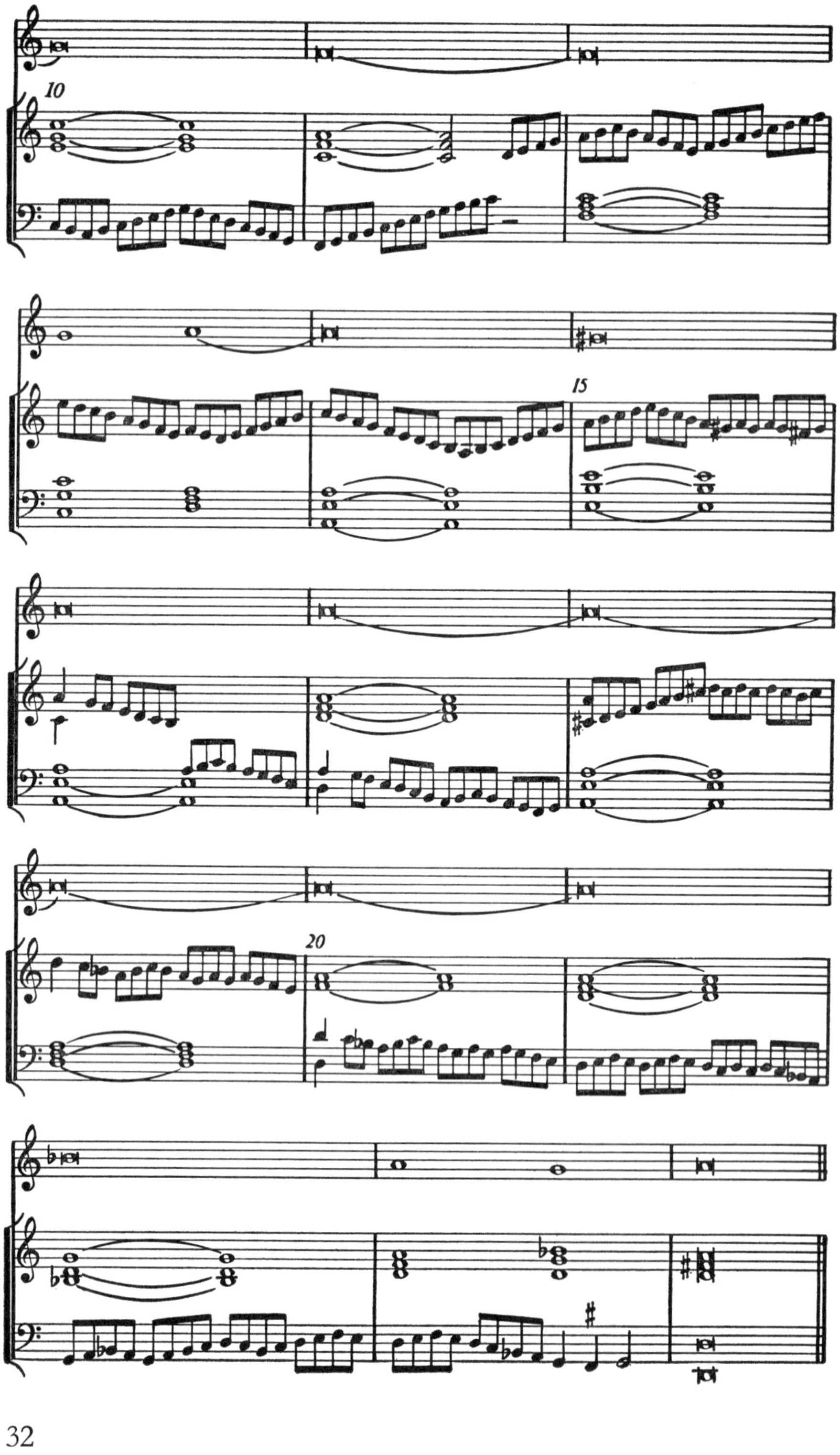
10
15
20

Despite this juggling of the original melody and other liberties, the inaudible *cantus firmus* is clearly present not only in Andrea's and Diruta's compositions, but also in those of Giovanni Gabrieli, Annibale, Bertoldo, Romanini, and Bell'Haver as well.

Other composers, though, began to place less emphasis on the single note recitation and more on the psalm tone cadence. Luzzaschi, for instance, does this in his toccata from *Il Transilvano* with the result that the "ideal" psalm tone becomes very difficult to trace, simply because its melodic contour has become more complex. Quagliati and Guami also began to introduce certain liberties in their treatment of the borrowed tones.[7]

Merulo, perhaps the greatest of all these composers, not only relied on the cadential melody of the Gregorian tone but often repeated parts of the borrowed melody. Unlike Andrea Gabrieli, he employed a fast harmonic rhythm and short figurations; moreover, he passed these from voice to voice much more quickly than Andrea did with his longer ideas, gaining through such means an intense kind of musical expression. The basis of the structure, however, remains the idealized psalm tone which Merulo presented in the opening measures of the following example (9) no less than three times. Although his toccatas, as well as those by other Venetian composers, may at first glance appear "somewhat helpless and confused,"[8] they are, as all of these examples have shown, extremely well-ordered compositions.

---

[7] Quagliati introduced a lengthy passage in which the last two notes of the mediant or final cadence (the harmonies fit either) are repeated four times, after which a section occurs which has no relation to the psalm melody. Such writing shows growing maturity and freedom in the handling of the ideal melody. Guami, too, introduced a middle section in his toccata in which the final cadence is repeated several times.

[8] Carl von Winterfeld, *Johannes Gabrieli und sein Zeitalter*, II (Berlin, 1834), 105.

Ex. 9 Claudio Merulo, *Toccata*, tone V (*Toccate*, 1604), ed. by Sandro dalla Libera, II (Milan, 1959), 1 - 2.

It can be seen, too, that the toccata is not an improvisatory composition, at least not in the sense that the musician is creating something "unforeseen" ("in provisus") or something evolved on the spur of the moment ("ex tempore"). If the toccata is improvisatory at all, it is in the sense of "discantus super librum," that ancient practice of adding parts at sight to a given plainsong. It is also improvisatory in the decorations that grace the "harmonized" psalm tone. But the concept of free improvisation in the toccata must be greatly altered, for the composer or organist was guided throughout his composition by one of the most solid of all compositional techniques — a *cantus firmus*.

There are many reasons why composers thought to employ a falsobordone procedure in intonation and toccata. The psalm tones themselves were simple melodies, easily retained in the mind and familiar to choir and audience. They afforded the improviser-composer a lucid, well-balanced skeleton that his imagination could clothe with the living tissue of harmonic, motivic, and rhythmic invention. Furthermore, they had for centuries been associated with particular modes, an immense aid in creating pieces whose chief function was to provide the choir with a particular pitch.

In addition, because he thought of this borrowed melody in harmonic terms — that is, as a falsobordone — the composer did not need to search for harmonies. The harmonic basis of the toccata, then, is not a random one. It is even possible, in imitation of the isorhythmic and isomelic techniques of the medieval motet to analyze the toccata in terms of an "isoharmonic" structure, but with this one qualification: the ideal melody, although it greatly confines the harmonic choice of the composer, does not limit it entirely. In the selection by Merulo given above, for instance, the composer harmonized the final plainsong cadence (D-B flat-C-A) first with a D-B flat-G-C-D-F harmonic progression (measures 3-4), next with a simple B flat-F progression (9-10) and finally with a B flat-F-C-F sequence of chords.

The choice of harmonies, especially among earlier composers like Andrea Gabrieli or Annibale Padovano, follows the psalm tone *cantus firmi* so closely that the pattern of the particular chords cannot be regarded merely as a matter of chance or as a result of chordal formulae or modal clichés. The harmonies are just too closely linked to psalm tone melodies for such considerations to be valid. The Appendix at the end of this monograph is more than a transcription of the important *Intonationi* of 1593, for the clear presence of ideal *cantus firmi* in piece after piece by Andrea and Giovanni Gabrieli is ample proof of what these composers were doing.

To offer even further evidence for the presence of *cantus firmi* in these Venetian toccatas, a few more analyses may be added. For the sake of conciseness the following abbreviations will be used: Rec[a] = the psalm tone recitation for the first half of the tone; Med = the mediant cadence; Rec[b] = the recitation for the second half of the tone; Final = final cadence. The plainsong *differentiae* are also given (if necessary) and measure numbers are placed in parentheses:

1) Sperindio Bertoldo (toccata printed by Klaus Speer, ed., *Annibale Padovano (c. 1527-c. 1575) and Sperindio Bertoldo (c. 1530-1570), Keyboard Compositions* ["Corpus of Early Keyboard Music," 34; American Institute of Musicology, 1969], No. 12, pp. 52-53):
Tone VI: Rec^a (1) Med (2-4) Rec^b (4) Final (5-7)
Rec^a (8-9) Med (9-11) Rec^b (11) Final (12-15)
Rec^a (16) Med (17-18; repeated 19-21; the original edition of 1591 has a d-f-a chord on the third beat of bar 20, not a d-f-b-flat chord as in this modern edition; the psalm tone fits the d-triad) Recb (22) Final (22-24)
Rec^a (25) Med (26) Rec^b (26) Final (27-29)

2) Girolamo Diruta (toccata printed in Krebs, "Girolamo Dirutas 'Il Transilvano,'" *Vierteljahrsschrift für Musikwissenschaft*, VIII (1892), 384-385):
Tone II: Rec^a (1) Med (1-2) Rec^b (2) Final (3-7) Transition (8)
Rec^b (9-10) Final (11-13) Transition (14)
Rec^a (14) Med (15); repeated 16-17) Rec^b (17) Final (18-19) Transition (20-22)
Rec^b (23-24) Final (25-35; last two notes repeated 33-35)

3) Vincenzo Bell'Haver (printed in Torchi, *L'Arte musicale in Italia*, III, 179-182):
Tone If: Rec^a (1-7) Med (8-15) Rec^b (15-19) Final (19-20)
Imitative section (based on the repeated notes of the recitation, bars 20-43)
Rec^b (43) Final (44-48)

4) Andrea Gabrieli (a toccata from Diruta's *Il Transilvano* of 1593; printed in Valentin's *Die Tokkata* ["Das Musikwerk," 17; Cologne, 1958], No. 4, pp. 16-17):
Tone X = IVE
Rec^a (1-8) Med (9-11; repeated 11-13) Rec^b (13-14) Final (14-16)
Rec^a (17-20) Med (21-23) Rec^b (23) Final (23-30)

5) Claudio Merulo (a manuscript toccata; printed in Dalla Libera, *Merulo Toccate*, III, 1-4):
Tone II: Rec^a (1-2) Med (2-3) Rec^b (3) Final (4-6)
Rec^a (7) Med (7-8) Rec^b (8) Final (8-9)
Rec^a (9-10) Med (10-11) Rec^b (11) Final (12-13); the final cadence is repeated 14-23; 23-25 is a transition

passage; 26-28 repeats the final cadence again)
The composition ends with an imitative section based on the final cadence.

It is important, furthermore, to realize that at the end of the 16th century, the falsobordone was at the height of its popularity.[9] Even more to the point is the appearance in 1594 of the first embellished falsobordoni.[10] These are actually vocal counterparts or more precisely *the immediate vocal models* for the keyboard toccatas. The main difference between the two is very slim and springs less from structural differences than from the demands of the psalm text itself. To embellish the recitation in these vocal pieces would not only have unduly lengthened the composition (already long enough through the cadential figurations), but would also have obstructed understanding of the text, and so, for the most part, composers maintained the homorhythmic, syllabic declamation of the psalm tone during the recitation. Also (since singers do have to breathe), they kept the larger two-part division of the old melodies.

Nevertheless, the similarities between the vocal embellished falsobordone and the intonation-toccata are striking. In the following example from Bovicelli's treatise of 1594, the plainsong is given first (10A), followed by the unembellished (10B) and then embellished (10C) falsobordoni. The final result (10C) is obviously *a toccata texture*: block chords supporting an embellished line. In short, at the very time intonations and toccatas were appearing in print, embellished falsobordoni (vocal mirrors of these instrumental compositions) were at the peak of fashion.

Ex. 10 Ruggiero Giovanelli, *Falsobordone,* tone I (*Regole, Passaggi di Musica,* 1594), facs. ed. by Nanie Bridgman, *Documenta Musicologica* XII (Kassel, 1957), 78 and 80

A) Gregorian Psalm Tone ID

---

[9] For instance, two publications among many, Zachariis's *Patrocinium musices* of 1594 and Gardano's *Falsi Bordoni* of 1601, contain between them a total of 236 falsobordoni.
[10] In Giovanni Battista Bovicelli's *Regole Passaggi di musica* (facsimile edition, *Documenta Musicologica*, XII [Kassel, 1957]).

B) Choral Falsobordone

C) Embellished Vocal Falsobordone (three lower parts from [b])

Fecit potentiam in bra - chi - o su -

Thus, despite the liberties that writers like Luzzaschi and Merulo took, a direct line exists between the vocal falsobordone (both unembellished and embellished), the keyboard falsobordone, the intonation, and almost all Venetian toccatas published between 1591 and 1604. In all three instrumental genres, the composers strove to create a more sophisticated and continuous form by concealing the simple two-part division of the model. In intonation and toccata they even tried and, with complete success, managed to conceal the familiar *cantus firmus*.

Two questions regarding the origin of the toccata still remain. First, why employ psalm tones for "pitch-giving" compositions? It is well-known that the Gregorian melodies, although written in specific modes, do not necessarily end on the final note of the mode. In psalm tone I, for instance, only three of the ten endings correspond to the tonic of the dorian mode. The answer to this lies in the contemporaneous practice of choral falsobordone. In the last part of the 16th century, composers clearly preferred one ending for each mode. Thus, for a falsobordone written in tone I, they favored a final D triad and a key signature of no flats, for one in tone II a final triad of G with a signature of one flat (that is, they always transposed tone II up a fourth), and so forth. Exceptions did occur, but the general trend is readily evident: the falsobordone settings of psalm tones did not use a variety of terminations but were commonly restricted to one for each tone. In following a similar technical procedure, toccatas were likewise circumscribed tonally.

A second question concerns the total lack of theoretical comment on the toccata in the 16th century. Two reasons explain this. First, the genre appeared in printed form only in the last decade of that century, and it would not be at all unusual if theorists, who are by-and-large *post facto* commentators, chose to ignore the genre for some time. Second, even though toccatas were certainly composed well before the time they were published (Annibale Padovano, for instance, had died as early as 1575), the genre grew out of the practice of a particular group of musicians, namely the organists of St. Mark's in Venice. Under such circumstances there was little need to write about something that could more easily be passed on by word of mouth, that is from one organist to another. Furthermore, the Venetians and many of those who came after them were chiefly practical musicians not theorists. They were concerned with doing, and not explaining. Thus, only when the genre grew in popularity were compositions written down, and only when it spread to different cities and lands did theoretical comment appear.

Michael Praetorius, the Wolfenbüttel lexicographer and composer, first defined the toccata in his *Syntagma musicum*, III (1619). It is, he wrote, "like a praeambulum or praeludium which an organist, when he first plays on an organ or clavicymbalum, before starting a motet or fugue, fantasizes beforehand with simple individual chords and embellishments."[11] Here, *in nuce*, are some of the more commonly held ideas of toccata composition — that it is a prelude,

---

[11] "Toccata, ist als ein Praeambulum, oder Praeludium, welches ein Organist, wenn er erstlich vff die Orgel, oder Clavicymbalum greifft, ehe er ein Mutet oder Fugen anfehet, aus seinem Kopff vorher fantasirt, mit schlechten entzelen griffen, und Coloraturen etc." (facsimile edition, *Documenta Musicologica*, XV [Kassel, 1958], 25).

introduces a vocal piece, is customarily improvised, and that its style consists of embellished chords.

The importance of Praetorius for the present discussion is that these are the exact concepts many later historians and theorists were to seize upon. Christoph Demantius, for instance, in 1632 used practically the same words as Praetorius to describe the toccata: it is "a prelude which an organist before he begins a motet or fugue fantasizes beforehand."[12] A century later, Mattheson, in his book on melody, emphasized the imaginative quality of the toccata. "In instrumental music," he wrote, "one finds still another definite type — which unlike all the others, however, remains undefined — of I don't know whether I should say melodies or musical whims, to which category boutades, capricci, toccatas, preludes, ritornelli, etc. belong. Now even if they look as though one would improvise them, for the most part they are set down on paper in an orderly fashion, but hold so little to bounds and order that only with difficulty can one label them with any other name than 'flashes of good inspiration.' Thus, they are characterized by Imagination."[13] In *Der vollkommene Capellmeister* of 1739, Mattheson again stressed the whimsical character of toccata composition: "Whoever can introduce the greatest amount of artistic embellishment and the most originality ["seltensten Fälle"] does the best job." Then, referring to fugal writing, Mattheson contrasted such an "orderly and restrained" style with that which should be found in toccatas and fantasias: "The larger and smaller sections [of a toccata] do not have to be directly connected much less executed in an orderly

---

[12] "Toccata ist ein praeludium welches ein Organist ehe er ein mutet oder fugam angehet aus seinem Kopff vorher fantasiert" (*Isagoge artis musicae*, 1632; quoted by Erich Valentin, *Die Tokkata* ["Das Musikwerk," XVII; Cologne, 1958], 3).

[13] "Noch eine gewisse Gattung, ich weiss nicht, ob ich sagen soll, der Melodien, oder der musicalischen Grillen, trifft man in der Instrumental-Musik an, die von allen übrigen sehr unterschieden ist, in den so gennanten Fantaisies oder Fantasie, deren Arten sind die Boutaden, Capricci, Toccate, Preludes, Ritornelli etc. Ob nun gleich diese alle das Ansehen haben wollen, als spielte man sie aus dem Stege-Reiffe daher, so werden sie doch mehrentheils ordentlich zu Papier gebracht; halten aber so wenig Schrancken une Ordnung, dass man sie schwerlich mit einem andern Nahmen, als guter Einfälle belegen kann. Daher ihr Abzeichen die Einbildung ist" (*Kern melodischer Wissenschaft*, 1737, pp. 122-123).

fashion. Hence, those composers who labor at correct fugues in their toccatas and fantasias have no concept of the style at issue, to which nothing is so contrary as order and restraint."[14] In 1758, Jacob Adlung wrote that "when large toccatas are nothing but fantasias, preludes, and several different fugal movements, these toccatas, too, could be improvised."[15]

Thus, Praetorius's simple definition was even more curtailed as time passed. Only one idea of his remained constant (an idea that may very well have been buttressed by Frescobaldi's famous dicta on the performance of his toccatas,[16] as well as by the changing style and design of the toccata itself) — namely that the toccata was an improvisational composition, an idea far from being correct.

The question remains, then, as to why Praetorius mentioned neither the psalm tone basis of the genre nor the similarity between its techniques and that of the falsobordone. Two things may explain this. First, Praetorius was writing in 1619, when the Venetian procedure was not the only way of writing a toccata. The very words that follow the above definition testify to this: "However some use one style and some another — hence, to treat it extensively here is unneccessary, and besides I consider myself too insignificant to be prescribing something for this or that person."[17] Praetorius's unwillingness on the one hand to describe the different sorts of toccatas and on the other to lay down rules as to how one should

---

[14] "Wer die meisten künstlichsten Schmückungen und selteneste Fälle anbringen kan, der fährt am besten... Die Haupt-Sätze und Unterwürffe lassen sich zwar, eben der ungebundenen Eigenschafft halber, nicht ganz und gar ausschliessen; sie dürfen aber nicht recht an einander hangen, vielweniger ordentlich ausgeführet werden: daher denn diejenigen Verfasser, welche in ihren Fantaisien oder Toccaten förmliche Fugen durcharbeiten, keinen rechten Begriff von dem vorhabenden Styl hegen, als welchem kein Ding so sehr zuwieder ist, dem die Ordnung und der Zwang" (*Der vollkommene Capellmeister*; Documenta Musicologica, V [Kassel, 1954], 88).

[15] "...wenn die grossen Toccaten aus nichts bestehen, als aus Fantasien oder Präludien, und verschiedenen Fugensätzen, so können auch diese Toccaten aus dem Ermel geschüttelt werden" (*Anleitung zu der musikalischen Gelahrtheit*, 1758; facsimile in Documenta Musicologica, IV [Kassel, 1953], 752).

[16] See Apel, *Geschichte der Orgel- und Klaviermusik bis 1700*, 447-448.

[17] "Einer aber hat diese, der ander ein andere Art, davon weitläufftig zu tractiren allhier vnnötig, vnd erachte mich auch zu gering, einem oder dem andern hierinnen etwas fürzuschreiben," (p. 25).

write a toccata is unfortunate, for we are actually left with the vaguest of definitions even in spite of the great lengths the author goes in his discussion of the genre.

Second, Praetorius was writing primarily for a German audience, many of whom would have been unfamiliar with falsobordoni or at the least would have had little use for psalm tone compositions of any sort.[18] Thus he related the toccata to a species of composition that any German musician would know, namely the prelude. Although subsequent chapters will prove that toccata and prelude often had more in common than is usually supposed — more, that is, than style and function (although one of Kleber's compositions of 1524, a "Finale seu praeambolon," proves that preludes could function equally well as postludes) — the two genres are essentially different.

Unfortunately, historians have relied far too much on a theorist who by his own admission did not go into great detail about the genre. Doubtless Praetorius knew it quite well, for he continues his definition with these words: "although I have collected many fine toccatas by the most renowned Italian and Netherlandish organists and have also in my own simple and small way composed several of them for the purpose of publication, yet I have not for the moment wanted to do this for several reasons." Rather abruptly, then, Praetorius digresses and says that "the Italians, however, call them toccatas, in my opinion, for this reason: because 'toccare' means 'tangere, attingere,' and 'toccata' means 'tactus.' Thus, the Italians say 'toccate un poco,' that is, 'touch the instrument or play the clavier a little.' Therefore, toccata can well be defined as a striking or touching of the clavier"[19] — an etymological digression of doubtful importance, since both term and thing are often quite different from each other and explaining one does not always explain

---

[18] For a discussion of German falsobordone, see this author's Ph. D. dissertation, *The History of the Falsobordone from Its Origins to 1750* (The University of Chicago, 1969), 84-85; pages 70-71 below contain some reasons for the eventual abandonment of the *cantus firmus*.

[19] "Und ob ich zwar viel herrliche Tocaten von den vornembsten Italiänischen und Niederländischen Organisten zusammenbracht, auch selbsten nach meiner Einfalt und Wenigkeit etliche darzu gesetzet, in willens dieselbige im druck zu publiciren: So habs

the other. The term and thing known as "fauxbourdon" comes immediately to mind; although the music is relatively well understood, the exact meaning of the term has led to an almost endless line of articles and books each proposing its own interpretation of "fauxbourdon." The term "toccata" has not presented much of a problem for historians (in contrast to "fauxbourdon"), but the music can now be seen to have been far less understood than has been thought — and a partial explanation for this lies in the importance accorded Praetorius's far from complete definition.

The toccata derived from the intonation and like its forerunner was modelled harmonically after the psalm tone, ideally present in the soprano. What has been unanimously regarded as one of the first examples of idiomatic keyboard writing now stands revealed as an instrumental work based on a vocal model. Its entire structure and chief elements — harmonic sections and florid passage work — have their analogue in the embellished vocal falsobordone, and this is the specific kind of falsobordone that most immediately affected the keyboard toccata.

These conclusions, then, alter considerably the traditional view of the genre. It is not a "free" composition, since it has a *cantus firmus* and is based on a vocal model. It is not an improvisational composition, either, because the performer was following prescribed harmonies and melodies. Its structure is not a mere contrast between toccata-like passages and imitative sections, but rather a *cantus firmus* structure. Indeed, the imitative sections — although they allowed the composer to add a different musical texture to the whole, to vary the number of parts, to employ a slower melodic rhythm (together with a faster harmonic rhythm), and, in short, to expand the breadth of a composition without running the risk of tediousness — nevertheless were not essential to the Venetian toccata: Andrea Gabrieli employed them in exactly half of his six known toccatas,

ich doch noch zur zeit vmb gewisser Ursachen willen nicht zu Werck richten wollen.
"Sie werden aber von den Italis meines erachtens, daher mit Namen Toccata also genennet, weil Toccare heiss tangere, attingere, und Toccato, tactus: So sagen auch die Italiäner; Toccate un poco: Das heisst: beschlagt das Instrument, oder begreifft die Clavier ein wenig: Daher Toccata ein durchgriff oder begreiffung des Claviers gar wol kan genennet werden," (p. 25).

and, even though Merulo usually employed imitative or ricercar sections, many of these have been deleted in the manuscript copy of his works in the Turin library.[20] Finally, the modality of these pieces is not at all ambiguous, but is firmly rooted in the psalm tones (which at this time were clearly circumscribed with regard to their final note). When a composer wrote a "toccata of the first tone," he employed no key signature, ended with a D triad (unless he transposed the piece), and built his work on the first psalm tone — exactly as in a falsobordone. It was, as previous examples have shown, clearly defined in its modal character.

Such a genre could have originated only in Italy. The falsobordone was immensely popular there, more so than in any other country. As Bovicelli's treatise also reveals, embellished versions were equally in demand. Furthermore, it is the city of Venice that assumed leadership over all Italy in the creation of an outstanding organ repertoire toward the end of the 16th century. Vincenzo Galilei, for instance, in his *Dialogo della musica antica et della moderna* (1581), stated that only a very few people knew how to write and play keyboard music well. "Anyway," he continues, "I do not believe that there are more than four of them, among whom Claudio da Coreggio, Giuseppe Guami, and Luzzasco Luzzaschi should be numbered."[21] The fourth is Annibale Padovano, and all of the names listed by Galilei are noted Venetian composers of toccatas.

Girolamo Diruta, too, was apparently overwhelmed by the skill of Venetian organists, for in his *Il Transilvano* of 1593, he vividly described how, after wandering through many lands, he finally came "to the most illustrious city of Venice. Hearing in the renowned church of St. Mark's a contest of two organs being played

---

[20] See Dalla Libera, *Merulo Toccate*, I, 10, 35, and 39, and II, 2, 4, 7, 19, 30, 37-38, 51, 58, and 60. In the Turin manuscript only the chordal basis of Merulo's toccata on the eighth tone (printed in 1604) was copied (see Dalla Libera, II, 42).

[21] "Quelli come Annibale Padouano, che habbiano saputo ben sonare e bene scriuere; à comparatione del numero che ci è de sonatori di tasti, sono pochissimi; & in tutta Italia di che n'è copiosa piu che altra parte del mondo, non credo in modo alcuno che passino il numero di quattro, tra i quali si annouerano Claudio da Coreggio, Giuseppe Guami e Luzzasco Luzzaschi" (facsimile edition in *Monuments of Music and Music Literature in Facsimile*, Second Series, XX [New York, 1967], 138).

antiphonally with so much ingenuity and elegance that I was transported beyond myself, and being eager to meet those two great champions, I stopped at the door where I saw Claudio Merulo and Andrea Gabrieli approaching, both organists of St. Mark's. Having attached myself ["dedicato me stesso"] to them, I decided to emulate them, especially Signor Claudio. With his learning and my effort, I gave up my poor habits, keeping the good ones." Diruta added that his intention in writing *Il Transilvano* was "so that those desirous of such a skill might not fall into the errors into which I, with many others, fell."[22]

Clearly, Venetian organists had attained a preeminence far beyond their colleagues of other cities, a preeminence and standard of excellence, too, that was apparently fostered by the authorities of St. Mark's themselves, in spite of apparent restless ministers. Caffi has recorded that a disposition of 1564 stipulated that a priest who began singing before the organist had finished must pay one ducat as penalty. Ministers were admonished to wait "quieti et con patientia" until the organist had stopped playing.[23]

Toccatas, at that time and place, were the keyboard counterparts to the massive polychoral motets and the instrumental canzonas and ricercars of these Venetian masters. Just as these compositions, the genre was well grounded in a clear, translucent structure. An educated listener in St. Mark's would have been delighted and fascinated by the metamorphosis of a simple, choral composition into the brilliance and dynamism of a toccata by Andrea Gabrieli or Claudio Merulo.

[22] "ma che, auedutomi dell'errore nel quale mi giaceuo, mi risoluei d'uscirne, & cercando diuersi Paesi, finalmente venni in questa Illustrissima Città di Venetia, & sentendo nel famosissimo Tempiò di San Marco un duello di due Organi rispondersi con tanto artifitio e leggiadria, che quasi vscij fuor di me stesso, & bramoso di conoscere quei due gran Campioni, mi fermai alla porta, doue viddi comparir Claudio Merulo, & Andrea Gabrieli, ambedua Organisti di San Marco, a' quali dedicato me stesso, mi diedi à seguitarli, & in particolare il Signor Claudio, là doue egli con il sapere, & io con lo studio, lasciai l'uso cattiuo, apprendendo il buone; & questa è stata la principal cagione, che m'ha indotto à far questa fattica, acciò non incorrano li desiderosi di tal virtù ne gli errori, in cui io con molti altri cadei..." (p. 36).
[23] Francesco Caffi, *Storia della musica sacra nella già cappella ducale di San Marco in Venezia dal 1318 al 1797*, Vol. I (reprint of edition of 1854; Milan, 1931), 30-31. Reese gives the date as 1546 (*Music in the Renaissance*, 544).

CHAPTER III

THE KEYBOARD PRELUDE AND LUTE TOCCATA OF THE RENAISSANCE

The relation of falsobordone and toccata to the earlier keyboard preludes of the Renaissance must now be revaluated, for these compositions, the first of which appeared as early as 1448, are certainly similar in function to the toccata. Moreover, such authors as Ferand, Frotscher, and others have observed stylistic similarities between the two.[1] The question is, did the prelude influence the toccata and can it be considered a legitimate forerunner of the toccata?

In looking at the earliest preludes, those from the 15th century, the most striking element is the great variety of styles. For instance, Ileborgh's tablature of 1448 contains three different kinds of preludes, one in which a sustained bass supports a forceful and driving upper part, another in which the bass moves more quickly, and a third in which the two styles are combined. In Berlin MS 40613, the composer employed in one piece a series of homorhythmic chords followed by a section with a two-part texture and, in contrast to Ileborgh, placed all this in a metrical scheme. In the four works from Erlangen MS 554, the sustaining lower part is increased now and then to two parts and the freely-flowing upper line to two additional voices and even full chords. The composer of the prelude in Hamburg MS ND VI 3225 began with two voices in a note-against-note style and ended with the sustained bass technique, the first section being metrical, the last free. The selections in the Buxheim organ book, compiled around 1470, also present a varied picture: contrast of textures, differing number of parts, powerful

---

[1] See page 16, note 10.

monophonic passages, and repetition of rhythmic and melodic ideas.[2] At the same time, none of the 15th-century composers relied on a psalm tone. They conceived their preludes within a framework which favored diversity in style, sectionalism in structure, and to a great extent brevity in length.

The first German preludes of the 16th century appeared in two organ tablatures written around 1520, one by Leonhard Kleber (ca. 1490-1556), the other by Hans Kotter (ca. 1485-1541). In Kleber's preludes, although the diversity of style and sectionalism in structure of the previous century is often continued,[3] the composer has now and then added a new controlling device: the Gregorian psalm tone. Gustave Reese pointed out that Kleber's preludes are "more skilfully and clearly constructed" than those in the 15th century, and, in speaking of a "Praeambalum in Sol flat" (folios 73v-74), he noted that "here, in embryo, is the toccata."[4] Apel, too, observed the similarity between a prelude of Kleber's ("Praeambalum in sol," folios 65v-66) and the later Italian intonation and toccata.[5] Both works mentioned by these authors are based on Gregorian psalm tones, and it is not at all far-fetched to see in this new sense of form and structure the influence of these melodies. One example from Kleber will make this clear. It is a composition Apel had called the "artistic highpoint" of the preludes.[6] The influence of the 15th-century German prelude is seen in the sectional structure and the contrasts in texture and number of parts, but the remarkably concentrated use of the Gregorian psalm tone, not only as an "ideal"

---

[2] Willi Apel has transcribed the preludes — from Ileborgh's tablature to those in the Hamburg manuscript — in *Corpus of Early Keyboard Music* (hereafter CEKM), Vol. I (American Institute of Musicology, 1963). The preludes of the Buxheim organ book are transcribed and edited by Bertha Wallner in *Das Erbe deutscher Musik*, XXXVII (Kassel, 1958) and XXXIX (Kassel, 1959).

[3] Kleber's tablature contains at least five different kinds of preludes: (1) a basically chordal texture which the composer then embellished; (2) solo passage work alternating with chordal sections; (3) a homorhythmic succession of chords in steady rhythmic values; (4) *a2* compositions emphasizing imperfect consonances; and (5) one "prelude and fugue" type. Furthermore, the composer at times combined these various types within a single composition.

[4] *Music in the Renaissance*, 664.

[5] *Geschichte der Orgel- und Klaviermusik*, 207.

[6] *Ibid.*, 208.

cantus firmus but also as melodic material for the music itself, is new and forward-looking. The composer worked from three basic motives, one derived from the mediant cadence of the psalm tone (see brackets *a* and *a¹*), another from the intonation (bracket *b*), and a third from the final cadence (bracket *c*). Over the entire composition, the longest and perhaps best prelude in the tablature, lies the implicit melody of Gregorian psalm tone I:

Ex. 11 Leonhard Kleber, *Finale in re seu preambalon*
(*Tabulatur für die Orgel*, 1524), f162v-f163

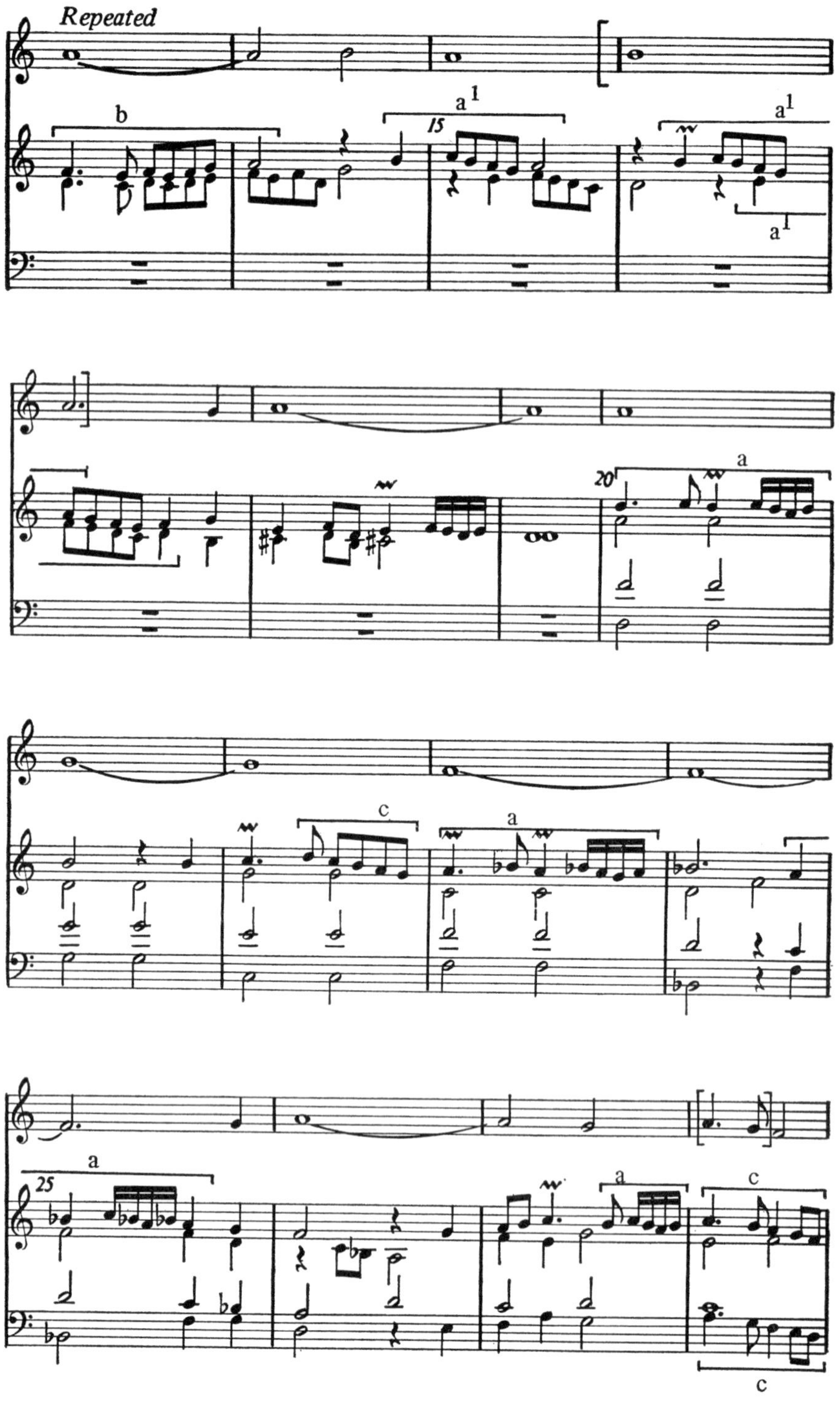
Repeated
b
a 1
15
a 1
a 1
20
a
c
a
25
a
a
c
c

* The bass note is *d* in the manuscript.

An even clearer illustration of Kleber's use of psalm tone *cantus firmi* can be found in his *Preambalon in La* (folios 68v-69), a piece which although it comes to several rhythmical halts nevertheless is unified by a single presentation of psalm tone IV:

Ex. 12 Leonhard Kleber, *Preambalon in La* (*Tabulatur für die Orgel*, 1524), f68v-69

* The *a* in the tenor voice is a semibreve (whole note) in the manuscript.

But why did Kleber and not the 15th-century composers of preludes turn to the old Gregorian psalm tones? The answer must be that the 16th-century composer was responding to more than just the psalm tone. He was shaping his compositions under the influence of the choral falsobordone that was just then beginning to appear in the very area where he worked, Southern Germany.[7]

Hans Kotter, an older contemporary of Kleber, also was intimately familiar with the genre. For many years, Kotter has been organist to Frederick the Wise in Torgau, the very place where between 1510 and 1520 the largest collection of pre-Reforma-

[7] For a brief discussion of this influence see the author's dissertation, *The History of the Falsobordone from Its Origins to 1750*, 85.

tion German falsobordoni was assembled.[8] His compositions, as Kleber's, have much of the past in them, but many reveal a solid foundation in the Gregorian melodies. For instance, Kotters "anabole [= prelude] in fa" is shaped around psalm tone V; after presenting the first half of the borrowed melody (measures 1-6), the composer started another recitation (7-10) and then proceeded to repeat the mediant melody several times and to change the texture (11-17), devoting the final four measures to the last half of the *cantus firmus*:

Ex. 13 Hans Kotter, *Anabole in fa* (Organ Tablature, ca. 1520), ed. by Wilhelm Merian, *Der Tanz in den deutschen Tabulaturbüchern* (Leipzig, 1927), pp. 62-63

[8] The manuscript is Jena, Choirbook 34. For information on its date and provenance see Christiane Engelbrecht, "Die Psalmsätze des Jenaer Chorbuches 34," *Kongress Bericht Köln* (Kassel, 1959), pp. 97-99. K. E. Roediger gives the musical incipits and a listing of contents in *Die geistlichen Musikhandschriften der Universitätsbibliothek Jena, Notenverzeichnis* (Jena, 1935). Wilhelm Merian transcribed Kotter's preludes in *Der Tanz in den deutschen Tabulaturbüchern* (Leipzig, 1927).

The psalm tone never became the dominating influence with the prelude as it later did with the Venetian intonation and toccata. In nine preludes from Regensburg MS FK 21 (from the Benedictine monastery of Neresheim near Württemberg in Southern Germany), only three have a clear psalm tone basis, even though all nine reveal an *a4* texture, a continuous flow, and an embellished top part supported by sustained chords — characteristics that will be associated with the later toccata.[9] The following example (14) of tone V, for instance, is founded on an ideal *cantus firmus*. In the Polish tablature of Johannes of Lublin, compiled around 1540, most of the preludes have a psalm tone basis,[10] whereas the two compositions in Klagenfurt MS 4/3 are based on an imitative structure with no reliance at all on a psalm tone.[11]

Ex. 14 *Preambulum in Fa* (Regensburg, FK 21), ed. by Eberhard Kraus, *Cantantibus Organis,* IX (Regensburg, 1962), 4

[9] Modern edition by Eberhard Kraus, *Cantantibus Organis*, IX (Regensburg, 1962).
[10] Modern transcription by John Reeves White, CEKM 6/I (American Institute of Musicology, 1964).
[11] Modern edition by Ambros Wilhelmer, *Musik alter Meister*, IX (Graz, 1958).

Many later English preludes, such as those in the Fitzwilliam Virginal Book, follow other structural principles, too. But even English composers of Elizabethan and Jacobean times turned to the psalm tone structure. An example by William Byrd (1543-1623) makes this quite clear:[12]

Ex. 15 William Byrd, *Praeludium,* tone VIII (Fitzwilliam Virginal Book), ed. by J.A. Fuller Maitland and W. Barclay Squire, Vol. I (Dover republication of original edition of 1899; New York, 1963), pp. 83-84

[12] Reprint of the original modern edition of 1899 by J. A. Fuller Maitland and W. Barclay Squire in Dover Publications (New York, 1963).

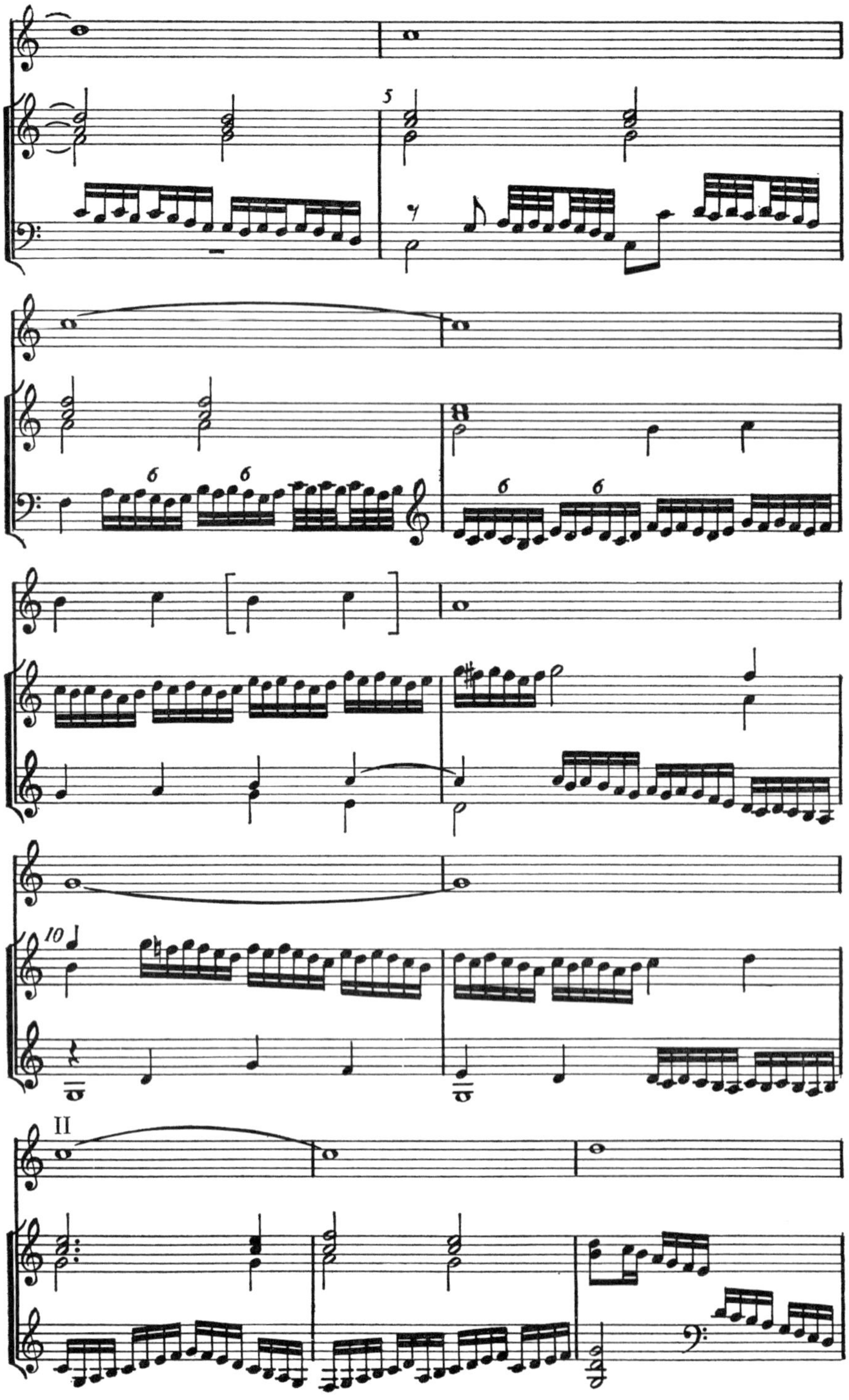
5
10
II

The single prelude in Pierre Attaingnant's *Treize motets* (1531) is a clear example of "ideal" *cantus firmus* treatment — the composer started with the last half of the psalm tone and then presented the entire tune with extensive repetition of the last two notes of both cadences — but the two preludes in his *Magnificat sur les huit tons* make no use of *cantus firmi*.[13]

Yet even though many of these preludes have much in common with the toccatas — not only an ideal *cantus firmus*, but occasionally even the texture and continuous structure — the greater length and breadth of the Venetian compositions stand out. It is an expansiveness fundamentally derived from the Italian composers' ability to develop the potentialities of the keyboard falsobordone. From this structure, they evolved a keyboard virtuosity completely and firmly rooted in the implicit and ideal *cantus firmus* of the Gregorian melodies. This remains the essential difference between toccata and prelude. The German prelude did not lead to the Venetian toccata, as is often suggested. Although inspired by choral and keyboard falsobordoni, composers were merely superimposing melodies on older devices in their preludes. Therefore even if a

---

[13] Yvonne Rokseth has edited both editions.

musician took up the new structural principle of a psalm tone *cantus firmus*, he was still tied to techniques and styles of the past, so far as the prelude is concerned. The toccata, on the other hand, grew out of a keyboard genre modelled directly on a vocal prototype to which the *cantus firmus* was organic.

Just as the German preludes, the various "toccatas" for lute preceded Venetian keyboard works by many decades. What is their relation to the Venetian toccata? Joanambrosio Dalza's collection, printed in 1508, contains five works labeled "tastar de corde," four of which are followed by a "ricercar dietro" ("ricercar afterward;" like the keyboard toccata, the genre acts here as a prelude). More to the point, however, is the discovery that Dalza employed a Gregorian psalm tone in these works, too. Here is the first toccata from his volume:

Ex. 16 Joanambrosio Dalza, *Tastar de corde,* tone II (*Intabulatura de Lauto,* 1508), ed. Johannes Wolf, *Handbuch der Notationskunde,* II (reprint of 1919 edition; Hildesheim, 1963), 54

Within this simple and concise piece, the composer presented the psalm tone twice, inserting only in measure 14 a harmony that does not fit the Gregorian melody, unless one wants to lengthen the b-flat and explain it as a cadential dissonance. Dalza, too, treated the borrowed theme ideally, using it as a basis for fresh melodies and harmonies. Another toccata by Dalza is a setting of the first psalm tone with the opening measures based entirely on the recitation note.[14] Although more expansive than the example given here, it still follows the same structural principle. Four "tochate" occur in Giovanni Antonio Casteliono's volume of 1536. In these pieces, too, the composer often employed a *cantus firmus*. Borrono's composition from this very same collection is founded on psalm tone IV.

Ex. 17 P.P. Borrono, *Thochata,* tone IV (Giovanni Antonio Casteliono, *Intabolatura de leuto,* 1536), ed. by Ernst Ferand, *Die Improvisation in der Musik* (Zürich, 1938), pp. 388-389

[14] Transcription in Adler's *Handbuch der Musikgeschichte*, I, 398-399.

Actually, it is not well known that falsobordone compositions exist for the lute. The following example by Francisco Guerrero (1528-1599), for instance, occurs in Miguel de Fuenllana's *Orphenica lyra* of 1554:

Ex. 18 Francisco Guerrero, *Falsobordone* for lute and voice, tone IV
(Miguel de Fuenllana, *Orphenica lyra,* 1554)

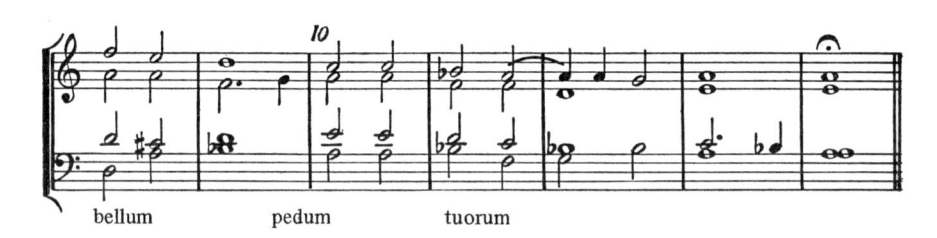

Although the text appears beneath the music, there is a question as to just what notes were intended to be sung. However, if psalm tone IV is superimposed over the above composition, the resulting melody seems to be exactly what the composer had in mind.

Sometimes, as in the next illustration (19), Guerrero has taken such extraordinary liberties with the form (note the imitative introduction, the instrumental interlude between both halves of the verse, the occasional reduction of the number of voices, and even the avoidance of repeated chords and notes), that it is only because this falsobordone is grouped with simpler ones that we recognize it as a member of the genre — proof that even such an apparently "free" composition is solidly grounded on a psalm tone *cantus firmus*.

It must be pointed out, too, that Guerrero's falsobordone could very well have been performed without the vocal part since, as noted above, the composer simply wrote the text under the tablature itself, not on a separate staff. Thus, the *cantus firmus* would truly be an ideal one. This lends support to the presence of inaudible melodies in early lute toccatas as well as in preludes. It means also that composers employed this technique not only throughout the 16th century but also in a wide variety of compositions — keyboard and lute toccatas, preludes, and falsobordoni for lute, as well as in the later ground-bass pieces already mentioned.

Guerrero's last composition (Ex. 19) is exceptional, for most lute falsobordoni remain close to the vocal paradigm. Thus, although the earliest lute toccatas appeared decades before lute falsobordoni, the two cannot be connected as cause and effect. Lute falsobordoni grew directly out of their vocal models, just as the keyboard falsobordoni did. Nor did lute toccatas lead to keyboard toccatas. What occurred here was also taking place in the prelude: vocal falsobordoni were being performed more and more and the concept of using a psalm melody in instrumental compositions was undoubtedly given impetus. Furthermore, not all lute toccatas have this ideal melody, nor are they at all uniform. Finally, the later toccata is solidly founded on an idiomatic style of keyboard playing, one that logically developed from the keyboard itself. It is the keyboard falsobordone, together with the embellished vocal falsobordone, that were the direct models for the Venetian toccata.

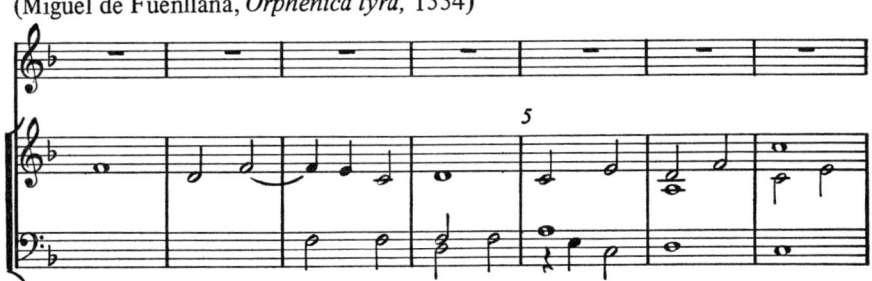

Ex. 19 Francisco Guerrero, *Falsobordone* for lute and voice, tone V
(Miguel de Fuenllana, *Orphenica lyra*, 1554)

64

All this leads, of course, to a radical change in our conception of 16th-century instrumental music, for many preludes, lute and keyboard toccatas, which formerly were thought to be "free" compositions, must now be considered *cantus firmus* compositions, pieces built on pre-existing melodies. The number of "free" works in the 15th and 16th centuries, then, is considerably less than previously had been thought. This new concept accords well with what we know of the Renaissance artist who seldom let his desire for expressiveness and individuality reign unchecked. On the contrary, he balanced them with clarity, logic, and order. In the intonation and toccata this control was furnished by the falsobordone and in many preludes and lute toccatas by a Gregorian psalm tone.

CHAPTER IV

TOCCATA AND PRELUDE IN THE SEVENTEENTH CENTURY

All the previous discussion raises a final question. Toccata and prelude continued to be important genres in the 17th century, especially in Austria and Germany. Just how long, then, did the Venetian structure survive and what is the relation of these later compositions to their prototypes, the 16th-century toccata and prelude?

No one disputes the Italian influence on the toccatas of Jan Pieterszoon Sweelinck (1562-1621, organist in Amsterdam). But with our new point of view, this influence can now be seen to extend far beyond that of style, for Sweelinck did in fact build all of his thirteen known toccatas on a psalm tone. A perfectly clear example is his setting of tone I where even the imitative section is based on the plainsong, a favorite procedure of the Venetians:[1]

Ex. 20 Sweelinck, *Toccata,* tone I, ed. by Max Seiffert, *Sweelinck Werken voor orgel en clavecimbel* (Amsterdam, 1943), 90-91

[1] Max Seiffert has edited the thirteen toccatas in *Sweelinck Werken voor orgel en clavecimbel* (Amsterdam, 1943). A toccata on the third tone by Pieter Cornet (ca. 1560-1626, organist at the court chapel in Brussels) uses the final ending of psalm tone III for the first ten measures only (see Willi Apel ed., CEKM, Vol. 26, No. 7, pp. 51-52); the remainder of the composition does not follow the Venetian structure.

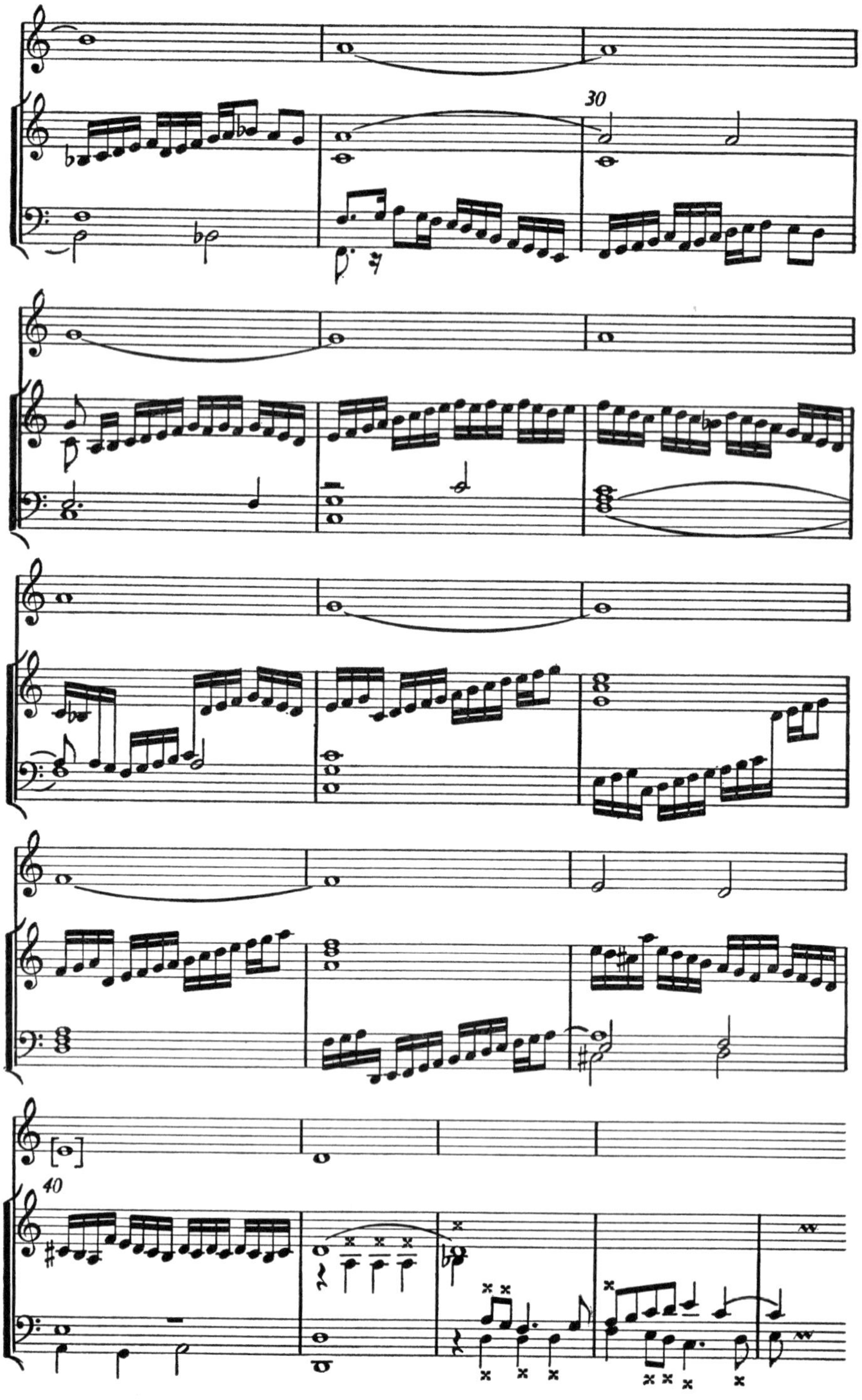
30
40

In every one of his toccatas, the old Venetian structure plays an important role, even though there are some sections where the *cantus firmus* is absent.[2] This means that another link exists between Sweelinck and Venice, and one very bit as substantial as style. It means, too, that the Venetian toccata, and hence the falsobordone, played a significant part in the history and development of German organ music, for from this Dutch (not "deutsche") "Organistenmacher" came pupils "who were to become the leaders of the northern baroque organ school which culminated in Johann Sebastian Bach."[3]

Among Sweelinck's more illustrious pupils in northern Germany was Samuel Scheidt (1587-1654, organist at Halle), whose three manuscript toccatas follow the pattern of his teacher not only in style but in structure.[4] For instance, at the conclusion of a piece on the second tone, Scheidt repeated the final half of the psalm tone three complete times:

Ex. 21 Scheidt, *Toccata,* tone II, ed. by Harms and Mahrenholtz, *Samuel Scheidt Werke,* V (Hamburg, 1937), 12

---

[2] As in tone IV (No. 21 in the ediiton mentioned above), tone II (No. 25), tone VIII (No. 27), in which the opening is unclear, as it is in No. 29, a setting of tone IV, and tone V (Nos. 31 and 32).
[3] Robert L. Tusler, "Master Jan Pieterszoon Sweelinck, Phoenix of Music," *Delta*, II/4 (1959-60), 76.
[4] The three toccatas are printed in *Samuel Scheidt Werke*, V (Hamburg, 1937).

Another toccata by Scheidt, one "super 'In te, Domine, speravi'" from his *Tabulatura nova*, III (1624), is quite unusual and deserves some explanation. Based on a brief *a3* canonical setting of psalm 70 (the first half of verse 1), the toccata is actually a set of variations.[5] Scheidt probably labeled it "toccata" because some of the variations have the artistic traits of Venetian pieces (solid chords supporting a decorated line) and unlike his usual variations the work has a continuous rather than sectional structure. Although a unique piece, it is significant that Scheidt, educated in the Venetian tradition, wrote a "toccata" that was explicitly based on a vocal composition and one, moreover, that was a setting of a psalm text.

It is equally significant that the number of his toccatas is considerably less than Sweelinck's and, indeed, that he saw fit to publish only one toccata. One reason is that Venetian toccatas

[5] For a discussion of Scheidt's several settings of this text see Christhard Mahrenholz, *Samuel Scheidt sein Leben und sein Werk* (Leipzig, 1924), 13-14 and 43-44; one of the canons is printed by Mahrenholz on p. 13. Max Seiffert has edited the toccata in *Denkmäler deutscher Tonkunst*, Vol. I (Leipzig, 1892), No. 12, pp. 147-151. A canon on the same text is found beneath Scheidt's reproduction in the *Tabulatura nova*; the same piece is transcribed as one of the canons at the end of the first part of the collection, just as the "toccata" concludes the second part.

were closely allied to the singing of psalms (either in plainsong or as falsobordoni) and the old Gregorian psalm tones, a link which Scheidt as organist in a Lutheran church had little reason to follow. His teacher Sweelinck was far closer to the Catholic religion and to Venetian practices than was Scheidt.

A second explanation for the abandonment of Venetian procedures is that newer structures and techniques were coming to the fore which furnished composers different tools for building up a composition. For instance, a toccata by Heinrich Scheidemann (ca. 1596-1663, organist in Hamburg) includes "echo" sections, a favorite technique of his teacher Sweelinck. A *präambulum* from the Lüneburg organ tablature KN 208[1] (dated 1630-1670) is an incipient "prelude and fugue," even though the composition is obviously modeled on the Venetian toccata structure.[6] Thus, despite the presence of psalm tone II in the first half and the composer's ingenious derivation of the fugal or ricercar subject from this tone (see asterisks in the following example), the composition is far removed from Venetian paradigms. The emphasis here is on a new, concise structure rather than the earlier, more expansive one:

Ex. 22 Anonymous, *Präambulum*, tone II (Lüneburger Orgeltabulatur KN 2081), ed. by Margarete Reimann, *Das Erbe deutscher Musik*, XXXVI (Frankfurt, 1957) 71 - 72

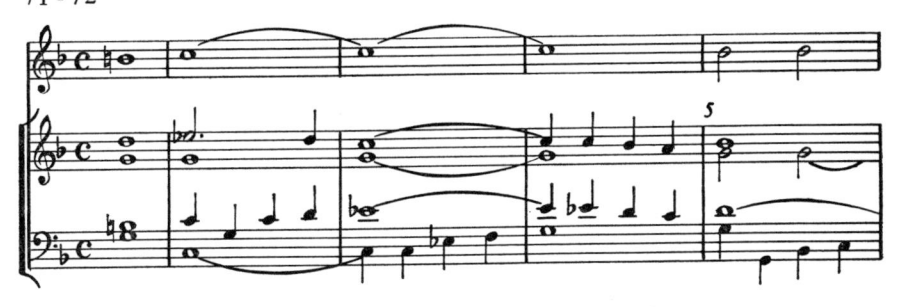

---

[6] Scheidemann's composition as well as the präambulum are edited by Margarete Reimann in *Das Erbe deutscher Musik*, XXXVI (Frankfurt, 1957). Some organ chorales by Scheidemann are transcribed by George Golos and Adam Sutkowski, CEKM 10/II.

In Southern Germany, the toccatas and "introiti" (the term seems related to "intonazioni") of Adam Steigleder (1561-1633, organist at Ulm), Hans Leo Hassler (1564-1612), Jacob Hassler (1569-1622), and Christian Erbach (1573-1635) — the last three of whom were at various times organists in Augsburg — clearly followed Venetian models.[7] Southern Germany had known the Italian falsobordone from the early 16th century on and cultivated it well into the 17th century. Also, the cultural ties between that area and Venice were many; from 1566 to his death in 1575 Annibale Padovano worked at Graz as organist and chapel master at the court of Prince Charles, Archduke of Austria; Andrea Gabrieli was a close friend of Orlando di Lasso and the teacher of Hassler; he also had connections with the Fugger banking family of Augsburg and dedicated many of his publications to Bavarian and Austrian princes;[8] Andrea's nephew, Giovanni, was active at the court of Munich from 1575 to 1579 and at a later date became the teacher

---

[7] Leo Schrade included a transcription of a toccata by Adam Steigleder in "Ein Beitrag zur Geschichte der Tokkata," pp. 633-635. Ernst von Werra has edited toccatas and *introiti* by Hans Leo and Jacob Hassler and Christian Erbach in *DTB*, IV/2 (Leipzig, 1903).

[8] See, for example, Giacomo Benvenuti's catalogue in *Andrea e Giovanni Gabrieli e la musica strumentale in San Marco* ("Istituzioni e monumenti dell'arte musicale italiana," Vol. I; Milano, 1931), Nos. 1, 6, 12, and 13, pp. XCVII, XCIX-CI.

of Heinrich Schütz. Other examples could be given, but it is clear that German and Austrian composers would be most susceptible to the Italian style and technique of toccata composition. In the opening of a "toccata II. toni," for instance, Hans Leo Hassler stays very close to the melody of the second psalm tone, particularly the second half of it, which he presents four times (exactly as Scheidt did in his setting of the same tone), after which he employed the entire tune and then began an imitative section.[9] The absolute clarity of technique as well as the importance of Hassler as a composer warrant the following extensive quotation of the opening bars of his toccata on the second tone:

Ex. 23 Hans Leo Hassler, *Toccata,* tone II, ed. by Ernst von Werra, *DTB,* IV/2 (Leipzig, 1903), 119-120

[9] *DTB,* IV/2, 119-120.

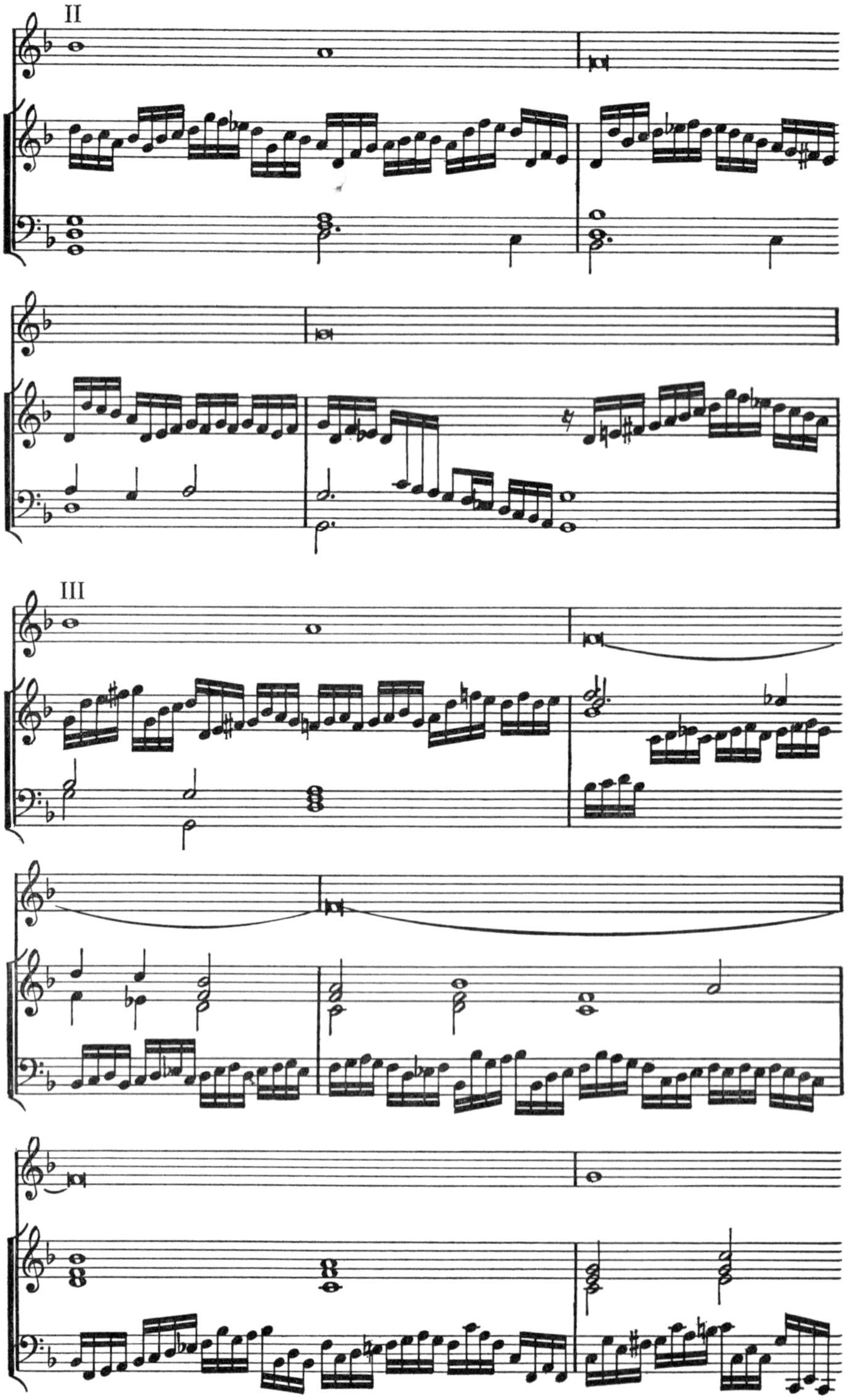
II
III

The "zwölff toni oder modi utraque scala" ("twelve tones or modes in both scales," that is, transposed and untransposed) by Samuel Mareschal (1554-1640, active in Basel) also followed Venetian models, except that the composer shunned brilliant embellishments.[10] The shortness of his works, as well as the presentation of each

[10] Transcribed by Jean-Marc Bonhote, *CEKM*, XXVII (American Institute of Musicology, 1967).

tone in an untransposed and transposed version remind us of Giovanni's compositions. There can be no doubt that Mareschal built the following "tonus" on psalm tone V:

Ex. 24 Samuel Mareschal, *Quinti toni, transpositus,* ed. Jean-Marc Bonhote, *CEKM* XXVII (1967), 5

* The e^1 is in the modern edition.

In the first half of the 17th century, then, composers of Northern and Southern Germany eagerly accepted the musical idiom and structure of the Venetian toccata, even though new forces were at work altering the older practice. During this time, too, Italian composers wrote toccatas. Yet among Neapolitan artists — Jean de Macque (ca. 1550-1614), and his students, Ascanio Mayone (d. 1627) and Giovanni Maria Trabaci (d. 1647) — the genre played a smaller role than in Venice. De Macque's only surviving toccata is "a modo di Trombette," and even though it includes sections with solid chords and decorative scale passages in the Venetian style it is clearly the broken, fanfare-like chords that capture our attention.[11]

Mayone's second publication of 1609 includes only five toccatas, and these differ in many ways from Venetian works of the preceding decade: they are harmonically more daring, more sectional in structure; the rhythms, too, are more complex than the Venetians', and the number of parts is occasionally reduced from the normal four to two or three; Mayone also inserted pure chordal sections alongside the traditional imitative and toccata-like ones. His works show a reaching out for new techniques, and only in a few of them — and here only for brief moments — is a *cantus firmus* present.[12]

Six toccatas by Ercole Pasquini (ca. 1560-ca. 1620, organist in Ferrara and Rome) survive. The composer built all six on a psalm tone *cantus firmus*.[13] Yet the number of his toccatas pales into insignificance when compared to the more than fifty compositions of this sort written by Italy's most renowned composer of keyboard music at this time, Girolamo Frescobaldi (1583-1643). With their frequent changes of harmony, tonality, melody, and rhythms, as well as their sectional structure, Frescobaldi's compositions belong unmistakably to the early Baroque; only a few reveal an ideal *cantus firmus* structure.

It would be naive, however, to say that Frescobaldi's apparent disdain for the older Venetian procedure was due entirely to a change in style from Renaissance to Baroque, although this had a great deal to do with it. An even more obvious reason is that his toccatas had a different function, one in which psalm tone *cantus firmi* were not involved. In his *Fiori musicali* (1635), a collection of three organ Masses and some incidental pieces, toccatas occur at three different places. First, the "chromatic" compositions were "per le levatione," to be played at the elevation of the Host, a most

---

[11] Printed in *Monumenta Musicae Belgicae*, 4e Jaargang (Amsterdam, 1938), pp. 67-68.
[12] Macario Santiago Kastner has edited the five toccatas from Mayone's *Secondo Libro di Diversi Capricci Per Sonare* (Naples, 1609), in *Orgue et Liturgie*, LXV (Paris, 1965).
[13] W. Richard Shindle has transcribed Pasquini's toccatas in *CEKM*, XII (American Institute of Musicology, 1966).

solemn and awe-inspiring moment in the liturgy. For this the composer chose a suitable style of music, one quite distinct from the lengthy, technically impressive Northern style.[14] In his two toccatas "before the ricercar," Frescobaldi again had little need for Venetian techniques. The ricercar itself was to be played "dopo il Credo" ("after the Credo"). The purpose of the introductory piece here was most likely one of transition. In effect, they are preludes to the Offertory (during which the ricercar was performed), the first part of the "Mass of the Faithful," just as the toccatas "avanti la Messa" are preludes to the "Mass of the Catechumens." Thus, the toccatas before the ricercar linked not only Credo to Offertory, but also the teaching portion of the Mass to the sacrificial part. Again, liturgical considerations predetermined musical style. Even in his three toccatas "before the Mass," Frescobaldi preferred a brief sort of composition, most likely to balance the toccatas that would appear later in the service. In any case, none of the toccatas in his *Fiori musicali* — neither those played "before the Mass," "after the Credo," nor "at the Elevation" — were associated by liturgical position with a psalm tone.

A second consideration is that many of Frescobaldi's other printed toccatas (1615 and 1627) were primarily intended for a clavier not an organ performance. None from the first collection is specifically labeled "per l'organo" nor is there any liturgical implication. Indeed, in the second book Frescobaldi identified two as "for organ" and two more as "with and without pedals," clearly implying that the remaining toccatas were neither limited to the organ nor to liturgical functions.

This is not to say that Frescobaldi never took up the Venetian procedure. He was, after all, a student of Luzzaschi (who had written a Venetian toccata for Diruta's *Il Transilvano*) and travelled widely in Italy and the north. But few of his toccatas follow completely the Venetian tradition. Now and then Frescobaldi took over

---

[14] A "toccata di durezze et legature" by Trabaci (1603) (printed in Torchi, *L'Arte musicale in Italia*, III, 370-371), is similar in style to these chromatic pieces by Frescobaldi; it does however lack imitative writing, a texture usually found in Frescobaldi's chromatic toccatas.

the psalm tone structure at the very beginning or end of a composition or even in the middle of a work,[15] but there can be no doubt that he made only a limited use of ideal *cantus firmi*. Michelangelo Rossi (ca. 1600-ca. 1674), a disciple of Frescobaldi, also made sparing use of the technique.[16]

Yet Venetian ideas had clearly swept to all parts of Europe. In addition to Sweelinck, the most remarkable appearance of the old Venetian technique occurs in the works of the peripatetic and influential Johann Jacob Froberger (1616-1667, court organist in Vienna). Practically all of his twenty-four toccatas open with a presentation of the psalm tone, after which the composer, by changing texture, rhythm, and melody, began a new and contrasting section.[17] The first measures of tone V make this abundantly clear:

Ex. 25 Johann Jacob Froberger, *Toccata,* tone V, ed. by Guido Adler, *DTOe,* X (Vienna, 1903), 16-19

[15] In the ninth and tenth toccatas from his first book, Frescobaldi made limited use of tones IV and V (see Pierre Pidoux ed., *Girolamo Frescobaldi Orgel und Klavierwerke,* III [Kassel, 1948], 32-39). In his second book Frescobaldi similarly employed a psalm tone in the fourth, fifth, ninth, and tenth toccatas.
[16] At the opening of six of his fourteen toccatas, Rossi employed a psalm tone. These pieces are transcribed by John R. White, *CEKM,* XV (American Institute of Musicology, 1966). A "toccata" from Giovanni Cavaccio's *Sudori musicali* (1626) is actually a polythematic ricercar (printed in Torchi, *L'Arte musicale in Italia,* III, 191-194).
[17] Edited by Guido Adler, *DTOe,* X/2 (Vienna, 1903).

But even in these sectional toccatas, Froberger extended the psalm tone structure well beyond the opening measures. In the second part of this work, the mediant cadence of the Gregorian melody supplies the melodic material for the quick give-and-take between all four voices (see asterisks in measures 12 and 13 of Ex. 25; the chordal outline of the melody, too, is reminiscent of the psalm tone intonation). The third part, with slowly moving harmonies and agitated melodic figures, again presents the "ideal" psalm tone for this mode. In the last part, it is the psalm tone intonation that provided Froberger with his melodic material.

Here, as in the second section, the psalm tone is not ideal, but is actually developed into melodic figures or motives. Froberger, in short, was doing exactly what the anonymous composer of the *präambulum* in the Lüneburg manuscript did: he kept the psalm tone procedure of the Venetians but placed it in a new context; he combined Venetian procedure with Frescobaldi's style and ornamentation. In his catholicity of style, Froberger is far more than a "deutsche Frescobaldi," as Schrade once labeled him, and his reliance on Venetian procedures has been completely underestimated.[18]

Johann Kaspar Kerll (1627-1683), another prominent member of the Catholic, Viennese circle, also followed the Venetian structure in the opening of his eight toccatas.[19] But with Kerll, the psalm tone does not pervade his compositions as it did in the works of Froberger. It is not found at all in the toccata from Alessandro Poglietti's "Rossignolo" suite. This work consists of four sections, all linked together and all contrasting in meter, tempo, texture, melody, and other traits; the composer made no use of a *cantus firmus*.[20]

The toccatas of later Viennese writers — F. T. Richter (1649-1711), Georg Muffat (1653-1704), Georg Reutter (1656-1738), F. X. A. Murschhauser (1663-1738), and S. A. Scherer (1631-1712; active at Ulm) — reveal both forward-looking and conservative elements. One by Reutter, for instance, bears no relation to the older design, whereas Richter clearly took it up in his single surviving example as well as in his ten "versets."[21] Georg Muffat, following the tradition established by Froberger, replaced the older Italian design with a suite-like structure, yet none of the twelve toccatas from his *Apparatus musico-organisticus* (1690) followed an "ideal" psalm tone. They were, indeed, free from *cantus firmi* of any sort.[22] The intonation and toccatas by S. A. Scherer make extensive use of pedal points, static harmonies, short melodic ideas, occasional

---

[18] Schrade, "Ein Beitrag zur Geschichte der Tokkata," p. 630. Other authors speak only of Frescobaldi's influence and not the Venetians' (see, for instance, Apel, *Harvard Dictionary of Music* [second edition, revised and enlarged; Cambridge, 1970], 853, and Bukofzer, *Music in the Baroque Era* (New York, 1947), 108.
[19] Adolf Sandberger has edited these compositions in *DTB*, II/2 (Leipzig, 1901).
[20] Modern edition by Hugo Botstiber ed., *DTOe*, XIII/2 (Vienna, 1906).
[21] *Ibid.*
[22] Modern edition by S. de Lange (Leipzig, 1888).

changes of meter and texture, as well as some fugal writing — but of no psalm tone *cantus firmi*.[23]

But Murschhauser, in an introduction to his publication of 1696, proves that one composer at least was still quite conscious of the old psalm tone melodies. "By no means," he wrote, have I unadvisedly omitted the obligatory bond ["obligationem"] of the *cantus firmi*, seeing that they can be, of course, appropriately applied not only to the Magnificat canticle but also to each of the eight psalm tones." Murschhauser added that "I have avoided the pretentious titles of toccatas and canzonas and, for the sake of simple uniformity, I have employed the name prelude and fugue, because I preferred to give the kernel of the matter without its shell, rather than the shell without its kernel." In this, as he stated, he followed the example of Kerll. Finally, the author decisively related these compositions to the psalm melodies when he said that the fifth tone is presented twice: "first on F-fa-ut with its natural termination on A-la-mi-re, just as it should regularly be placed; then in an irregular way so that it begins on C-sol-fa-ut and, moreover ends there."[24] Significantly, Murschhauser spoke first of the fifth tone on A (the final of the psalm tone and not the lydian mode) and then on C (the final of the fifth or lydian mode transposed down a fourth). Thus, over one-hundred years after the first toccatas had appeared in Venice, composers were still basing their works on old plainsong melodies. Yet Murschhauser did not employ these melodies as pervading and ideal *cantus firmi*, but, following the model of Kerll

---

[23] Modern edition by Pirro in *Archives des maîtres de l'orgue des XVIe. XVIIe. et XVIIIe siècles*, VIII (Paris, 1907).

[24] Obligationem tamen Cantus firmi haud inconsulto ibidem praetermisi, quatenus scilicet non solum Cantico Magnificat, sed cuivis ex. 8. Tonis Psalmorum adhiberi commodius possent. A gloriosis Toccatarum Canzonumque, titulis abstinui, sed simplici Praeambulorum ac Fugarum nomine, servandae uniformitatis gratia, usus sum, quia nucleum sine cortice, quam corticem sine nucleo dare malui; exemplum in hoc secutus famosissimi Musurgi, meique omni observantia colendissimi Magistri, Praenob. D. Joan. Caspari Kerll, p. m. cui quia totum debeo, totum, quod valeo, gratus reddo ... Caeterum invenies hic; Benevole Lector, Quintum Tonum duplici modo productum: primo in F-fa-ut, cum naturali sua terminatione in A-la-mi [-] re, prout regulariter poni deberet: deinde modo irregulari, ita ut incipiat in C-sol-fa-ut ac ibidem etiam definat; tum quia scio, tam profundam hujus Toni transpositionem apud nonnullos passim invaluisse" (*DTB*, XVIII, 78).

and to a certain extent Froberger, as sources for further melodic motives.[25]

Murschhauser's reluctance to use the term "toccata," because he desired to present the "kernel not the shell," is probably a reference to the small dimensions of his pieces. It may also obliquely refer to toccata composers of Northern Germany in the last of the 17th century. Here the tradition passed on by Sweelinck began to die out. The toccatas by Matthias Weckmann (1619-1674, organist at Hamburg) are quite independent of the older structure, although two of them bear some relation to tone I.[26] The same comment may be given for one toccata by Jan Adam Reincken (1623-1722, organist at Hamburg).[27] Other Northern composers — Dietrich Buxtehude (ca. 1649-1707, organist at Lübeck), Andreas Kneller (1649-1724, organist at Hamburg), Christian Ritter (ca. 1645-after 1724, organist at Halle, Dresden, Hamburg, and the Swedish court), and Nicolaus Bruhns (1665-1697, organist in Husum) — adopted a "prelude and fugue" structure. Unlike Murschhauser and other Southern composers, the works of these Lutheran composers are not linked in any way to a psalm tone.

In Central Germany, composers did not favor toccata composition. For instance, Johann Christoph Bach (1642-1703, organist in Eisenach and a cousin of Johann Sebastian's father) wrote at least forty-four organ chorales and a few variations, but no toccatas at all. Those of Johann Pachelbel (1653-1706, organist in Eisenach, Erfurt, Stuttgart, Gotha, and Nuremberg) are based on long pedal points with simple, slow-moving harmonies and brilliant figurations — another method for building a toccata but one which Murschhauser might have thought emphasized the "shell" (idiomatic

---

[25] For instance, the prelude on the first tone is derived from the final and mediant cadences of tone I, the first fugue from the intonation and final cadence, the second from the final, the third from the mediant, and the fifth from the intonation; the fourth fugue bears little relation to the psalm tone (five fugues and a finale follow each of the nine preludes). Tone I is printed *DTB*, XVIII, 79-80.

[26] Six toccatas by Weckmann are printed in *Organum*, IV/3 (Leipzig, n. d.). The opening measures of the first two compositions (pp. 32-37) are based on psalm tone I.

[27] The first part of a toccata in *Organum*, IV/5 (Leipzig, n. d.) seems based on tone VIII transposed down a fourth.

keyboard writing) rather than the "kernel" (the psalm tone structure). A toccata by Johann Kuhnau (1660-1722, Bach's predecessor at Leipzig) reveals the multipartite structure that many other Baroque composers favored, with no reliance at all on the psalm tones.[28] Those by Johann Krieger (1651-1735, organist in Bayreuth and Zittau) bring forth another formal element, one that more than any other brought the psalm tone influence to an end. This is the appearance of the major and minor tonalities. For instance, it is easy but overly facile to superimpose psalm tone V on Krieger's Prelude in F; what is most important is that the piece is in F major, and it is this tonal structure which primarily guided Krieger in his composition.[29]

Italian organists in the last half of the 17th century kept on using the Gregorian melodies in their works but seldom for entire compositions. For instance, Bernardo Storace, a Neapolitan composer, employed psalm tone VIII twice in one toccata, but only after a long and free opening section. In another toccata, the recitation and mediant cadence of psalm tone VI provided the structural framework for the last four measures. In contrast to Storace, Gregorio Strozzi, another Neapolitan composer, made no use at all of psalm tones in his four extant toccatas, nor for the most part did Bernardo Pasquini (1637-1710, active in Rome). Pasquini, however, employed a psalm tone occasionally at the opening of a composition, as did Alessandro Scarlatti in four of his multimovement toccatas. Even as late as 1716, Domenico Zipoli (1688-1726, active in Rome and Seville) was still employing the Venetian structure.[30]

All these compositions led ultimately to those by J. S. Bach. Not that, as one author has said, the development of the toccata from its beginnings to these later works is marked by an ascending

---

[28] Printed *Organum* IV/19 (Leipzig, n. d.).
[29] Max Seiffert has edited this work in *DTB*, XVIII (Leipzig, 1917), 37.
[30] Barton Hudson has transcribed Storace's two toccatas in *CEKM*, VII (American Institute of Musicology, 1965), and Strozzi's five toccatas in *CEKM*, XI (American Institute of Musicology, 1967); toccatas by Bernardo Pasquini were transcribed by Maurice Brooks Haynes in *CEKM* 5/V (American Institute of Musicology, 1967); ten toccatas by Alessandro Scarlatti are printed in *I Classici Musicali Italiana*, XIII (Milan, 1943). Zipoli's composition has appeared in *L'Arte musicale in Italia*, III.

line of excellence,[31] but simply that Bach was one of the last great composers who wrote a significant number of these pieces. The organ compositions of Johann Gottfried Walther (1684-1747, organist at Weimar), for instance, include a great number of chorale preludes, some concerto arrangements, a few preludes and fugues, but only one toccata and fugue (in which two pedal points, on the tonic and dominant respectively, hold the toccata together).[32] Georg Böhm (1661-1733, organist at Lüneburg) wrote mostly organ chorales together with suites and preludes and fugues.[33] In a publication of 1726, Gottlieb Muffat (1690-1770; active in Vienna) used several toccatas (all brief compositions of a single character or mood) to precede his versets on each of the tones.[34] Yet, the number of composers interested in the genre as a means of expression had clearly declined.

In his harpsichord toccatas, Bach favored a sectional structure, modern tonalities, mature fugal writing, harmonic richness, and all the other features we associate with his music. These features also appear in his organ toccatas; most are coupled to a fugue, and others — such as the toccata in C major (BWV 564) — have a sectional structure. Yet even though none of his toccatas, nor most of those by his contemporaries, follow the ideal psalm tone structure of the Venetians, they are inconceivable without these prototypes. Through such composers as Sweelinck and Froberger, the Venetian toccata had penetrated the musical life of Europe. Many composers gave up the *cantus firmus* structure — substituting for it other forms and techniques such as the prelude and fugue, or a series of short fughettas, or a suite-like arrangement, or lengthy pedal points, or modern tonality — but none abandoned the virtuosity and idiomatic writing that were an integral part of the first toccatas.

Yet to view the toccata solely as a technical display piece,

---

[31] Valentin, *Die Entwicklung der Tokkata*, 96.
[32] See the new revised edition of his works by Hans Joachim Moser ed., *DdT*, 26/27 (Wiesbaden, 1958).
[33] See Johannes Wolgast ed., *Georg Böhm Sämtliche Werke*, I (Leipzig, 1927).
[34] See *DTOe*, XXIX/2, Band 58 (Graz, 1960).

as the first instrumental form to record free improvisation, is no longer possible. Above all, it fails to account for the great emotional power found in toccatas from Merulo and Frescobaldi to Buxtehude and Bach.

From their very origin, toccatas were founded upon and controlled by liturgical *cantus firmi*. This underlay all other musical elements just as the sacred purpose of these early works contributed to their emotional depth. Even when this structure was abandoned, the serious, rhapsodic nature of the earliest compositions lingered on through the works of Bach, despite great changes in the means of expression. As important as virtuosity was, it was but an adjunct to a style and structure that dated back to at least the middle of the 16th century and had its roots in the decoration of a vocal composition. To understand the nature and meaning of the Baroque toccata, then, it is essential to remember that its origins lay in the singing of Vesper psalms in *a4* harmony.

APPENDIX OF MUSIC

A modern transcription of the *Intonationi* of 1593 needs little justification. The collection, which apparently was to be the first of several such volumes,[1] contains the first known examples of "intonations." It contains, too, toccatas by one of the very oldest members of the Venetian school of keyboard composers, Andrea Gabrieli (c. 1510-1586) as well as intonations by one of its youngest members, Andrea's nephew, Giovanni Gabrieli (1557-1613). It therefore affords us excellent insights into the close relation of intonation and toccata, just as it provides us with examples spanning a large period of time. Thus, printing such an anthology, rather than the works of an individual composer,[2] helps us, as one scholar has put it, "to perceive the [artistic] tradition in all its fullness,"[3] and not solely in the works of one man. Above all — and this is indeed the main purpose of the appendix — it allows us to see with the greatest clarity the technique of "ideal" *cantus firmus* writing as carried out by two of the finest keyboard composers of the Renaissance.

To make this procedure as tangible as possible, the ideal psalm tone melody is placed on a separate staff above the music. Certain abbreviations have been used:

Intr.	= introductory measures which affirm the modality (the harmony being the same as the final one) but are not based on the psalm tone.
Rec[a]	= psalm tone recitation for the first half of the tone.
Med	= mediant cadence.

---

[1] The title mentions that it is "Book One," implying other volumes were to follow: INTONATIONI D'ORGANO / DI ANDREA GABRIELI, ET DI GIO: SVO NEPOTE / ORGANISTI DELLA SERENISS. SIG. DI VENETIA IN S. MARCO / Composte sopra tutti li Dodeci Toni della Musica. / Nouamente stampate & poste in luce. / LIBRO PRIMO. / In Venetia Appresso Angelo Gardano / M. D. LXXXXIII.

[2] Giovanni's works from the *Intonationi* are edited by Sandro dalla Libera (Milan, 1956) and will also appear in Denis Arnold's edition of the complete works ("Corpus Mensurabilis Musicae," 12). Andrea's compositions are edited by Pierre Pidoux (Kassel, 1959). There are of course the older editions, Alexander Guilmant's of Andrea's intonations ("Archives des maîtres de l'Orgue des XVI.e XVII.e XVIII.e siècles," X) and Luigi Torchi's of Giovanni's intonations ("L'Arte musicale in Italia," III). Up to now the volume has not appeared as a complete edition.

[3] Edward E. Lowinsky, *Monuments of Renaissance Music*, I (Chicago, 1964), v.

Rec^b = recitation for the second half of the tone.
Final = final cadence.
Transition = a free section linking different presentations of the psalm tone.

Roman numerals refer to the repetition of the psalm tone (or a significant part of it); if there are no Roman numerals, the tune is presented only once. Notes in parentheses are melodic embellishments.

In looking especially at the intonations of Andrea, little doubt can remain that this composer consciously took up the psalm tone melodies as the basis for his pieces. In his intonations for tones I, IV, V, and VIII, he employed the Gregorian tones in a completely uncomplicated way, seldom repeating the theme or adding embellishing notes. The remaining intonations present varying degrees of complexity. In tone III, for instance, several embellishing notes are added to the ideal melody, and the final notes are repeated. Tone VI proceeds in a conservative fashion until measures 10-12 where some repetition takes place. In his settings for tones II and VII Andrea repeated the entire last half of the tone, a decidedly unusual procedure for such brief works.

Yet even when he does take up a somewhat more complicated *cantus firmus* technique, the borrowed melody remains clearly in the forefront of his creative thought. The same is true for Andrea's toccatas, though repetitions here become the rule and not the exception. His "toccata ... del Quinto tono" is a straightforward presentation of psalm tone V without one note of embellishment; at measure 12 the melody is repeated. The "toccata ... del Sesto tono" is more sophisticated: after three appearances of the plainsong melody (with a transition section separating each repetition), an extensive imitative part occurs (measures 27-57) which leads without pause to a fourth presentation of the melody. The "toccata ... del Nono tono" (employing psalm tone IV) is similar to the setting of tone V in its direct and simple use of a psalm tone (it appears six times); there is also an imitative section based on the repeated notes of the recitation. Of all the toccatas, that in tone VIII presents the greatest difficulties of analysis — until it is realized that the composer worked only with the first recitation and mediant cadence, and used these two segments no less than eleven times.

The collection opens with Giovanni's eleven intonations (the transpositions of these pieces are noted in this edition but not transcribed), a group of works that at first sight seem more conservative than those by his uncle. Yet, Giovanni not only sets tones IX through XII but also is far looser in his *cantus firmus* treatment than was his uncle. For instance, in the intonation "primo tono" he used only the last half of the Gregorian melody, a procedure employed also in tones II and VI. In tones IX (= IV) and XI (= V) he kept only the first half of the psalm tone. In tones VII,

VIII, and XII (= VIII) Giovanni relied on the entire psalm tone to hold his compositions together. The setting of tones III-IV is difficult to analyze although strong argument can be made for the presence of tone IV.

Such analysis, however important it may be, gives us merely the outline or frame of a composition. Most important is that this procedure was the springboard for a great and universal creative effort. If Andrea and Giovanni used such a technique, it is almost certain that other Venetians did, too — and hopefully this monograph has shown just that. It is also likely that other composers who came into contact with the Venetian school — such as Sweelinck and Froberger — would have taken it up although in different stylistic settings. The value of such a technique resides exactly in this fact — that it was serviceable for both an Andrea and a Giovanni Gabrieli, as well as for a Sweelinck and a Froberger.

INTONATIONI D'ORGANO

DI ANDREA GABRIELI, ET DI GIO: SVO NEPOTE

ORGANISTI DELLA SERENISS. SIG. DI VENETIA IN S. MARCO

Composte sopra tutti li Dodeci Toni della Musica

Nouamente stampate & poste in luce.

LIBRO PRIMO

In Venetia Appresso Angelo Gardano

M. D. LXXXXIII.

INTONATIONI DI GIO. GABRIELI

1. Primo Tono.[4]

2. Secondo Tono.[5]

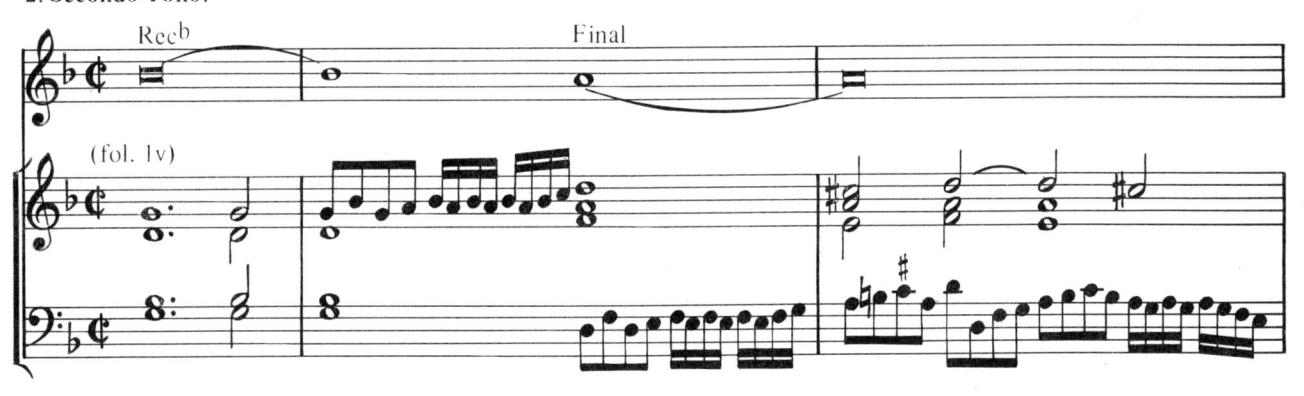

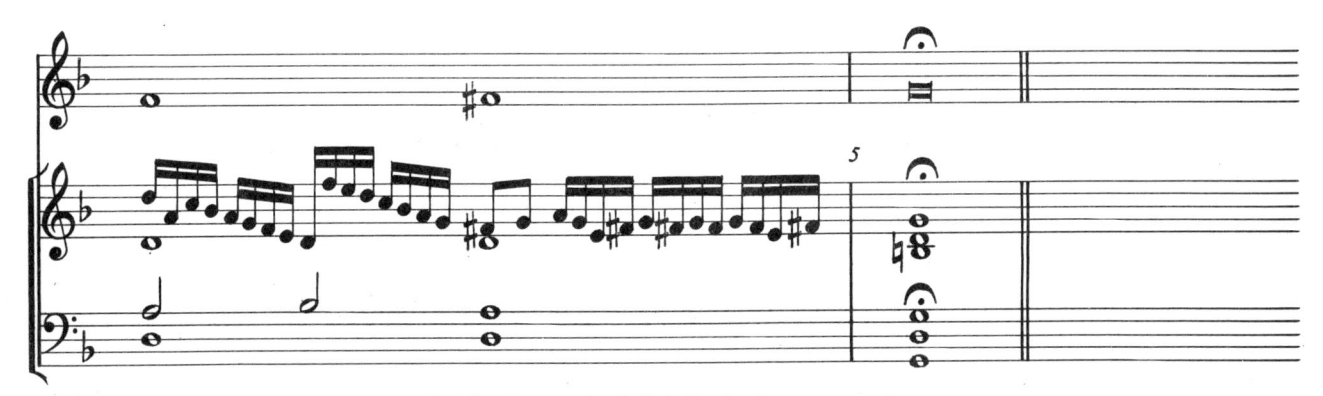

[4] Followed by "Primo Tono Trasportado alla Quarta alta," (fol. 1), that is, a transposition up a fourth with a key signature of one flat and ending on G.

[5] Followed by "Secondo Tono Trasportado alla Quinta alta," (fol. 2), that is, a transposition up a fifth with a key signature of no flats and ending on D.

3. **Terzo & Quarto Tono**[6] [Tone IV]

4. **Quinto Tono**[7] [transposed down a fourth]

[6] Followed by "Terzo e Quarto Tono Trasportado Alla Quarta Alta," (fol. 3), that is, a transposition up a fourth with a key signature of one flat and ending on A.

[7] Followed by "Quinto Tono Trasportado alla Quarta alta," (fol. 4), that is, a transposition up a fourth (actually the normal, untransposed position of the tone) with a signature of one flat and ending on F.

5. Sesto Tono[8]

6. Settimo Tono[10]

[8] Followed by "Sesto Tono Trasportado alla Quarta alta," (fol. 5), that is, a transposition up a fourth with a signature of one flat and ending on B-flat.

[9] Original: bass note *c* is a minim (half note).

[10] Followed by "Settimo Tono Trasportado alla Quinta Bassa," (fol. 6), that is, a transposition down a fifth with a signature of one flat and ending on C.

7. Ottauo Tono[11]

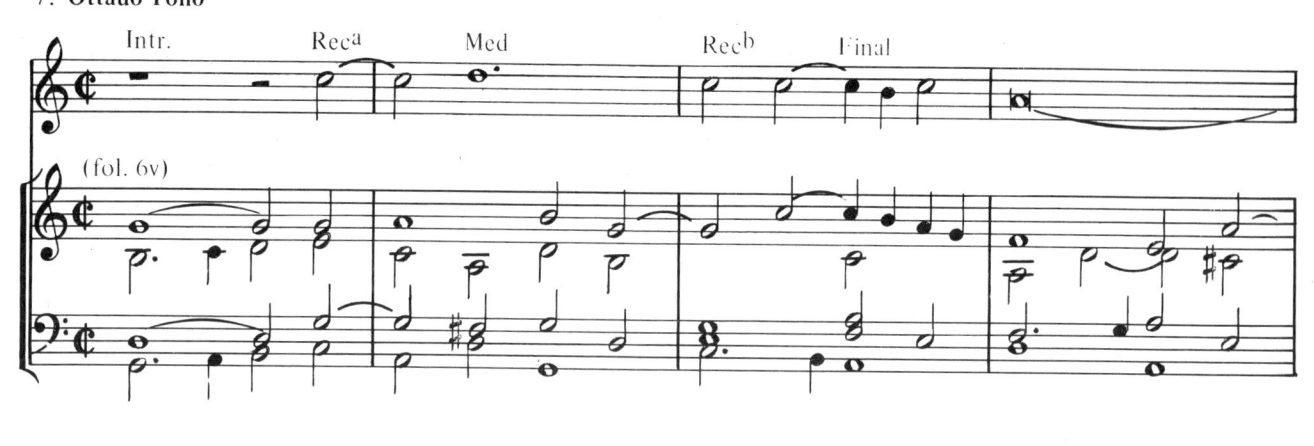

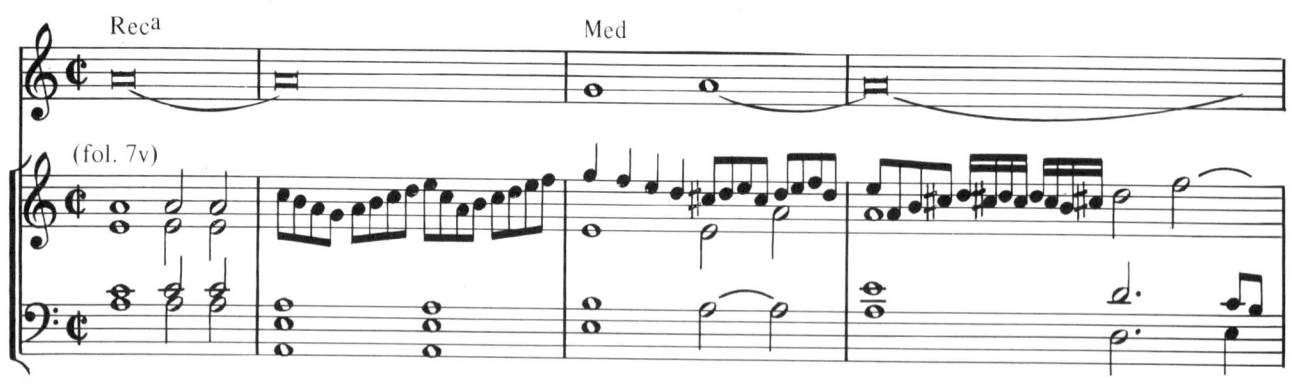

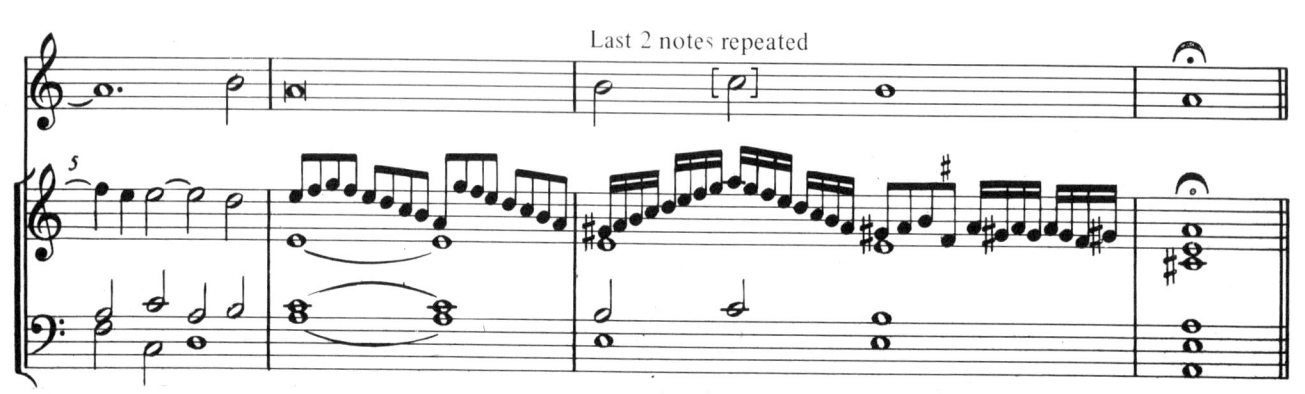

8. Nono Tono[13] [= IV]

[11] Followed by "Ottauo Tono Trasportado alla Quarta alta," (fol. 7), that is, a transposition up a fourth with a signature of one flat and ending on C.

[12] Original: tenor d^1 omitted.

[13] Followed by "Nono Tono Trasportado alla Quinta Bassa," (fol. 8), that is, a transposition down a fifth with a signature of one flat and ending on D (with incorrect clefs on the last line of the original).

9. Decimo Tono[14] [= IV]

10. Vndecimo Tono[16] [= V]

[14] Followed by "Decimo Tono Trasportado alla Quarta alta," (fol. 9) that is, a transposition up a fourth with a signature of one flat and ending on D.

[15] Original: bass note *a* omitted.

[16] Followed by "Vndecimo Tono Trasportado alla Quarta Bassa," (fol. 10), that is, a transposition down a fourth with a signature of no flats and ending on C.

[17] Original: second note from the top is *d²*.

11. **Duodecimo Tono**[18] [= VIIIG]

INTONATIONI DI ANDREA GABRIELI

12. **Primo Tono**

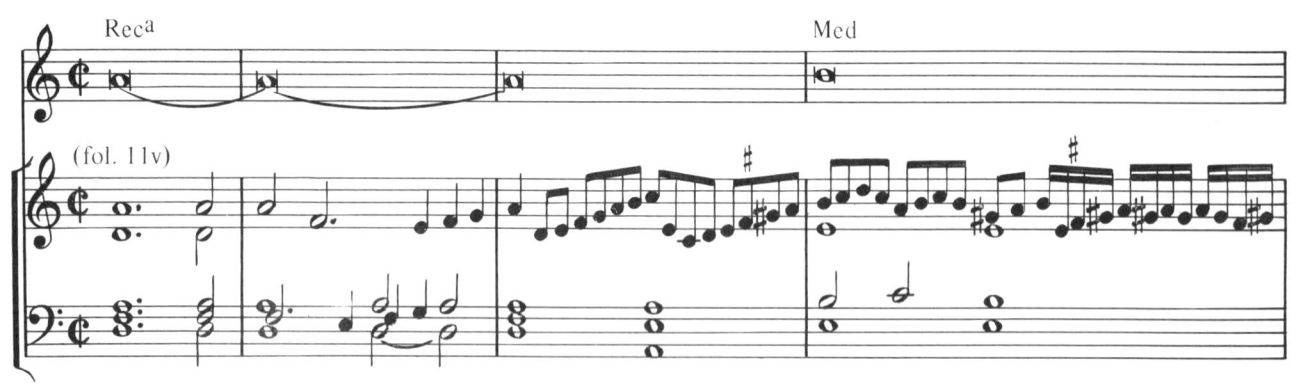

---

[18] Followed by "Duodecimo tono trasportado alla Quinta Bassa," (fol. 11), that is, a transposition down a fifth with a signature of one flat and ending on F.

[19] Original: rest omitted in bass.

13. Secondo Tono

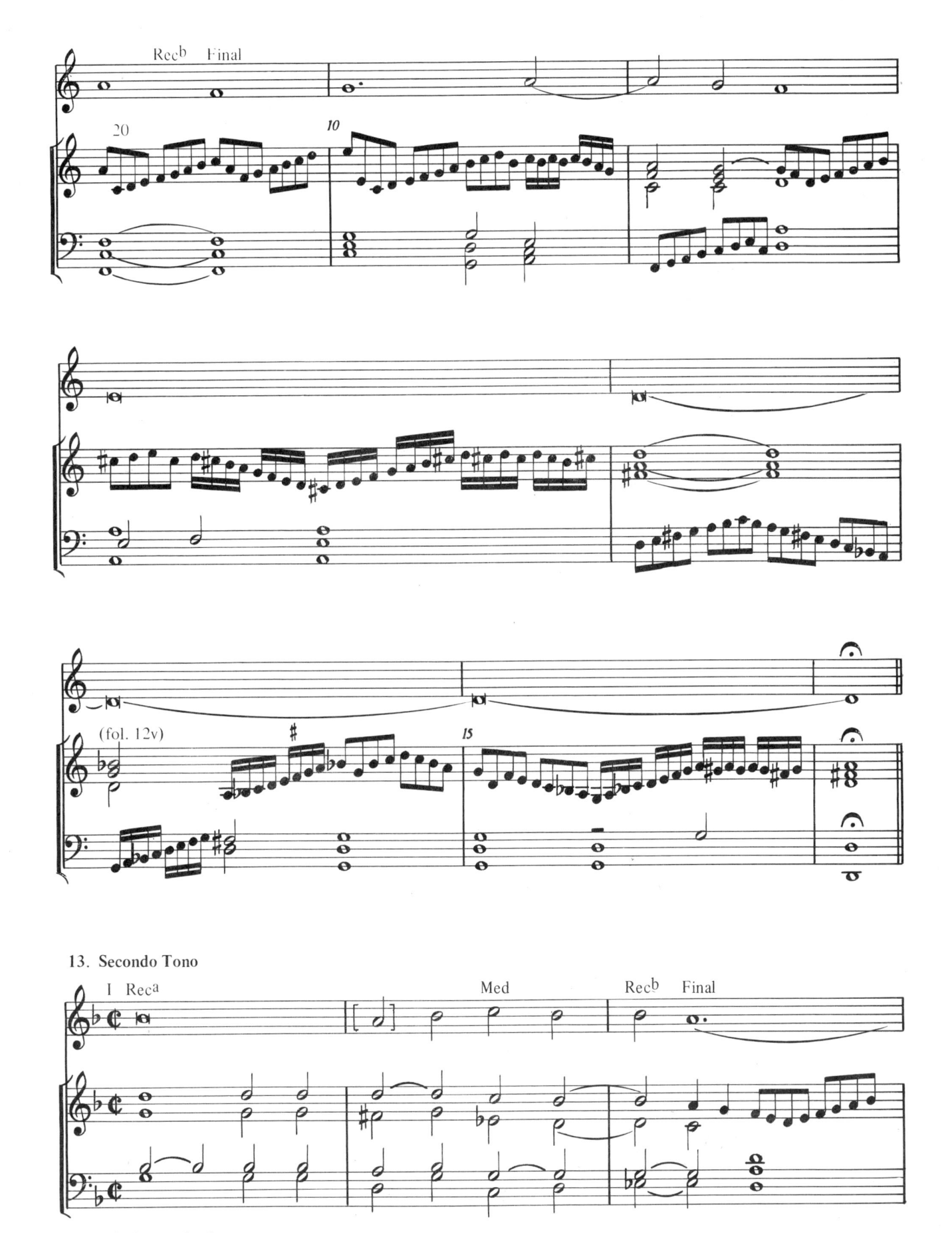

[20] Original: c^1 omitted.

14. Terzo Tono

[21] Original has two folios numbered 12.

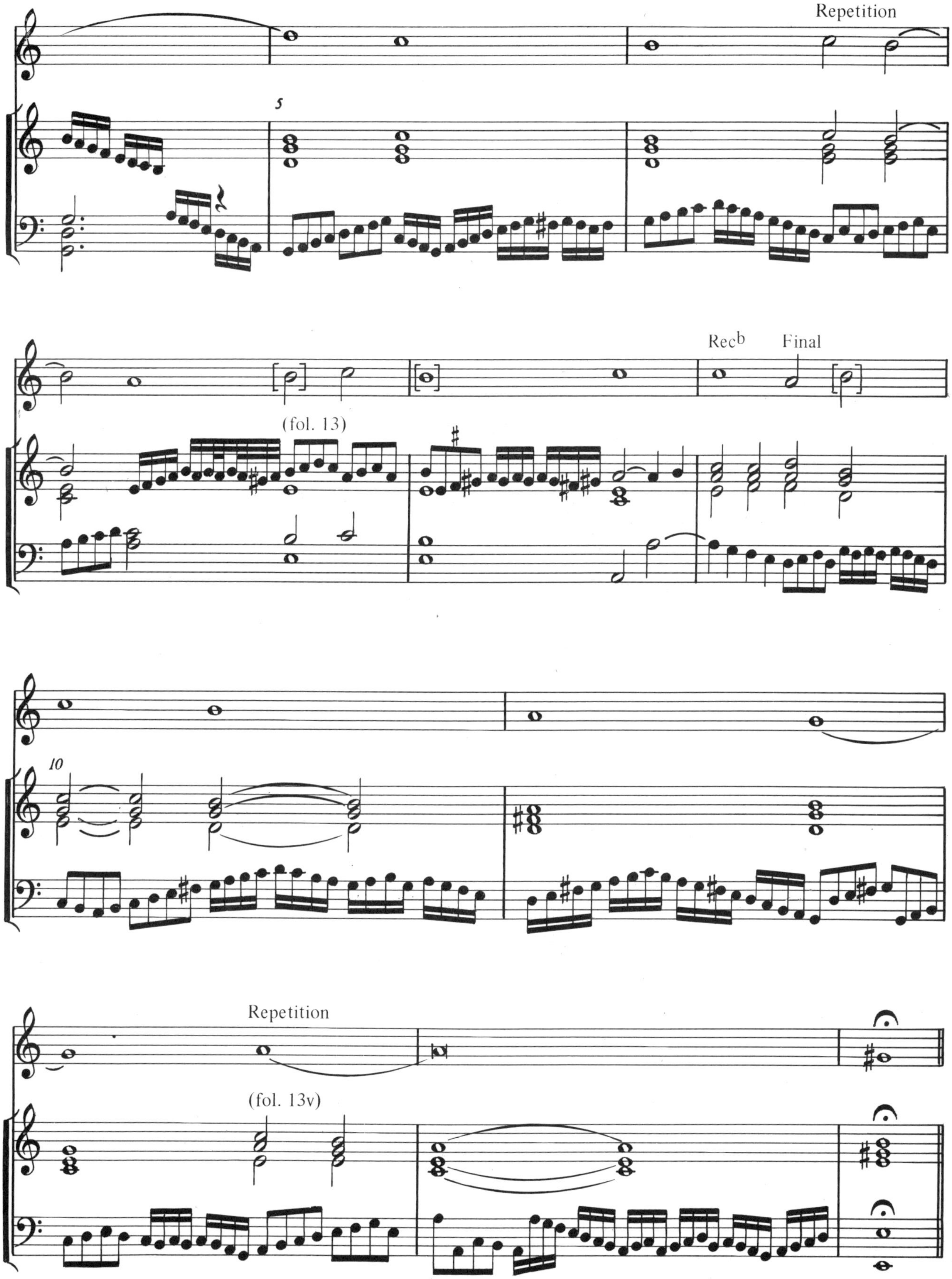
Repetition
5
Recb
Final
(fol. 13)
10
Repetition
(fol. 13v)

15. Quarto Tono

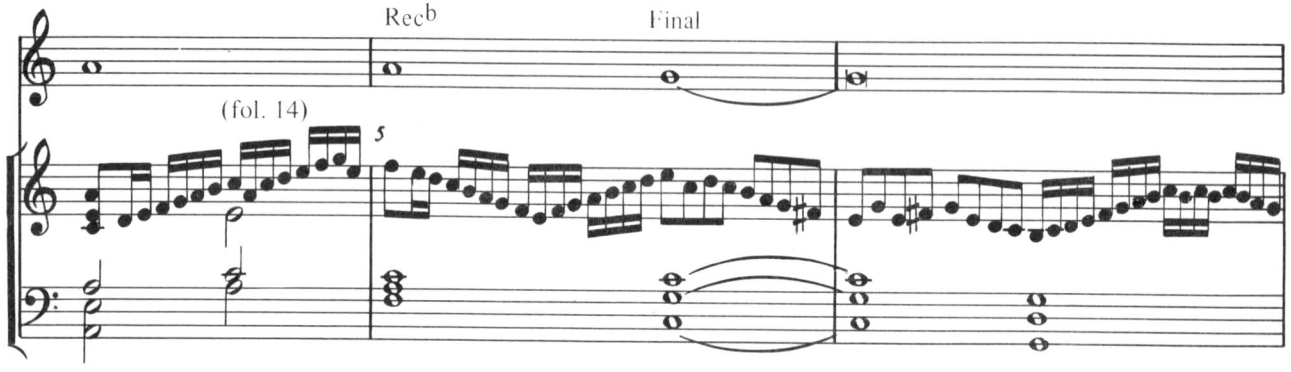

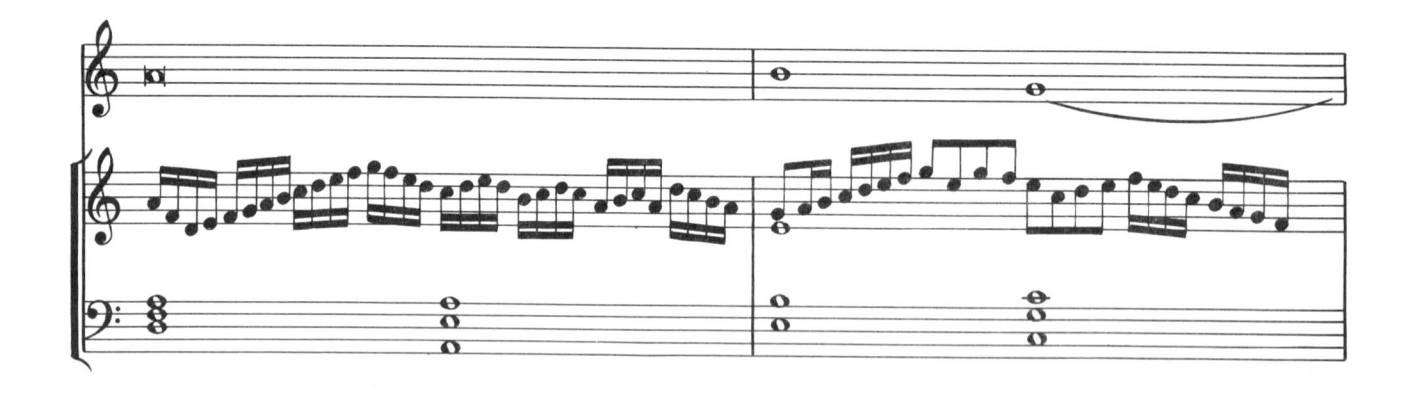

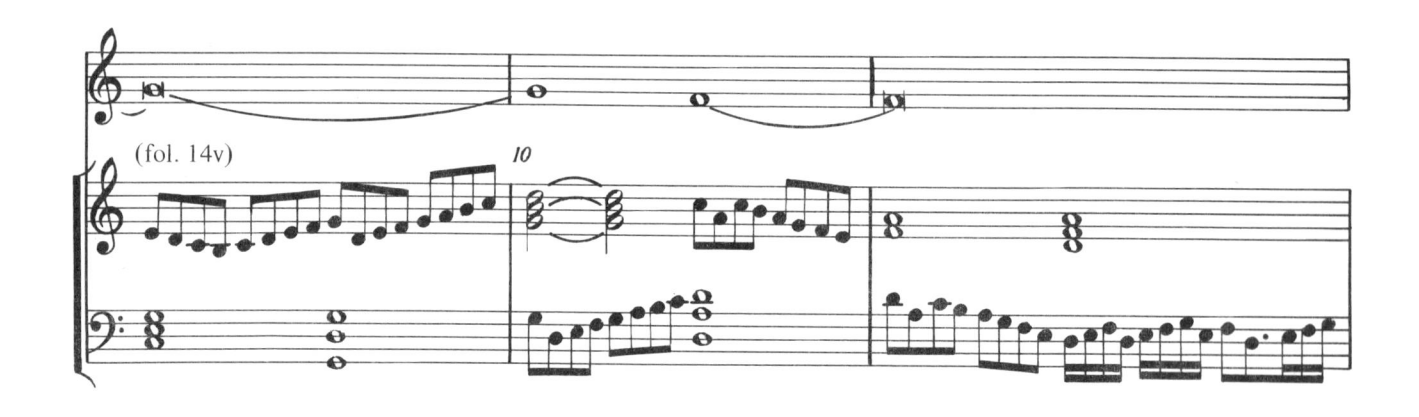

16. **Quinto Tono** [transposed down a fourth]

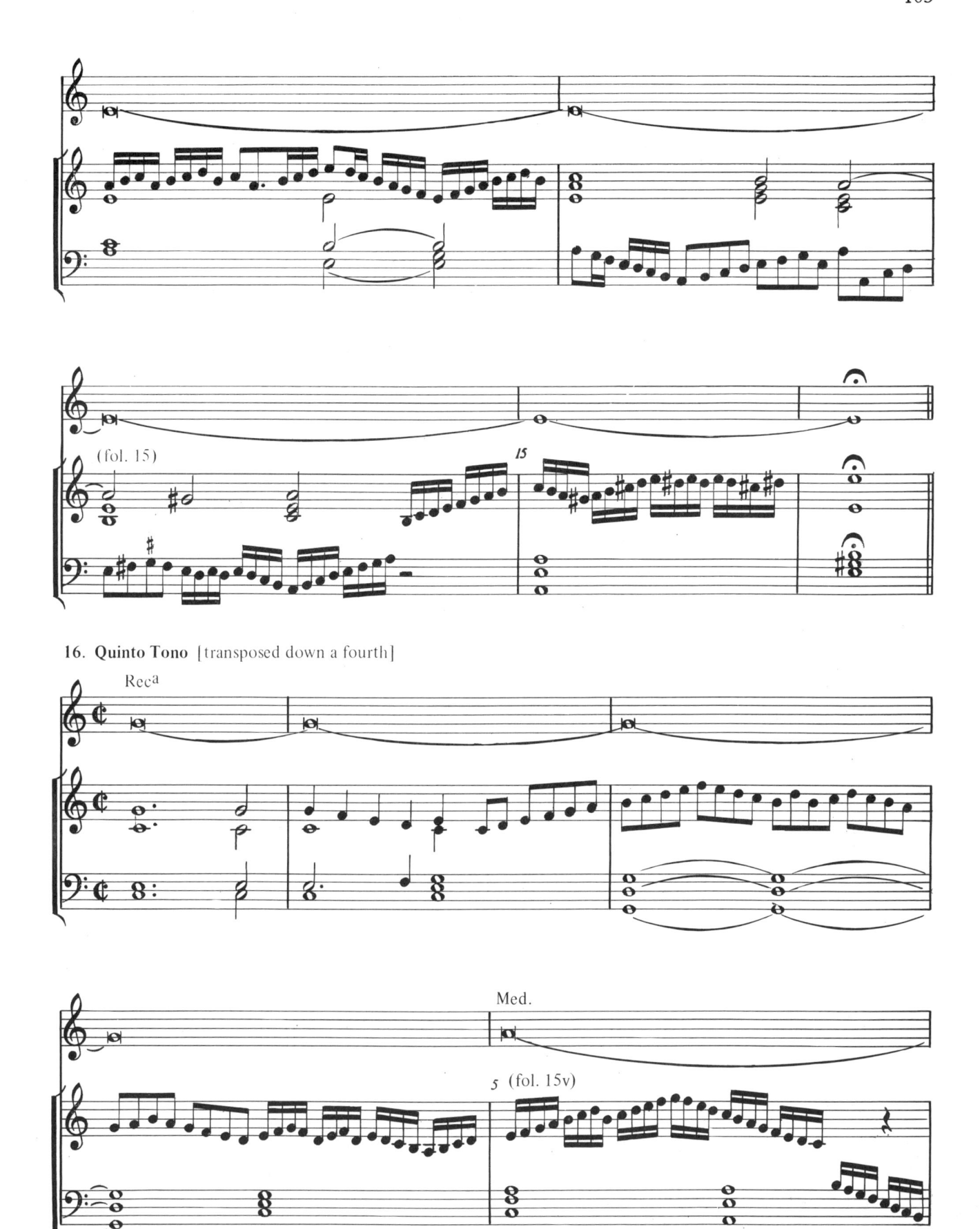

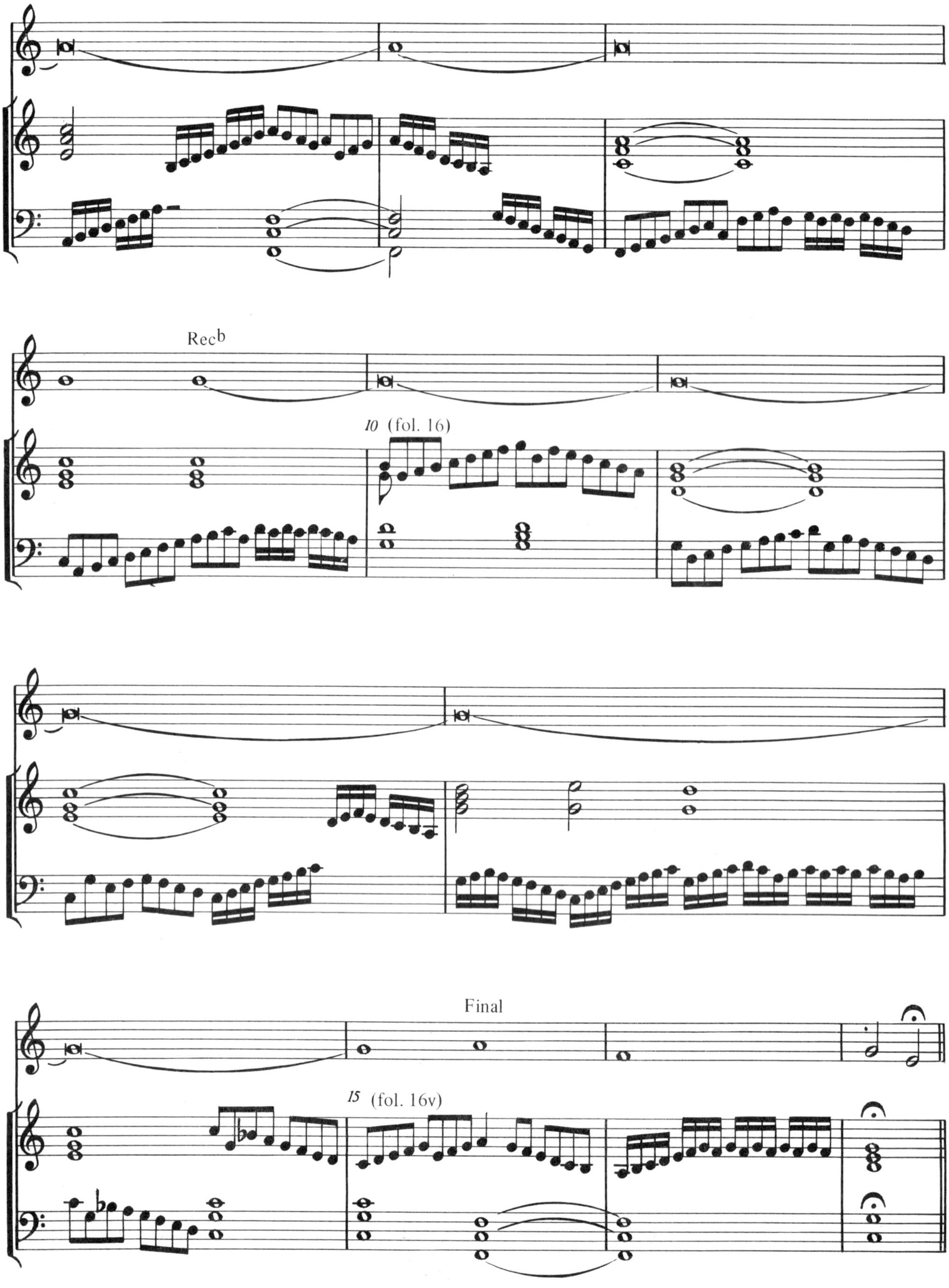
Recb
10 (fol. 16)
Final
15 (fol. 16v)

105

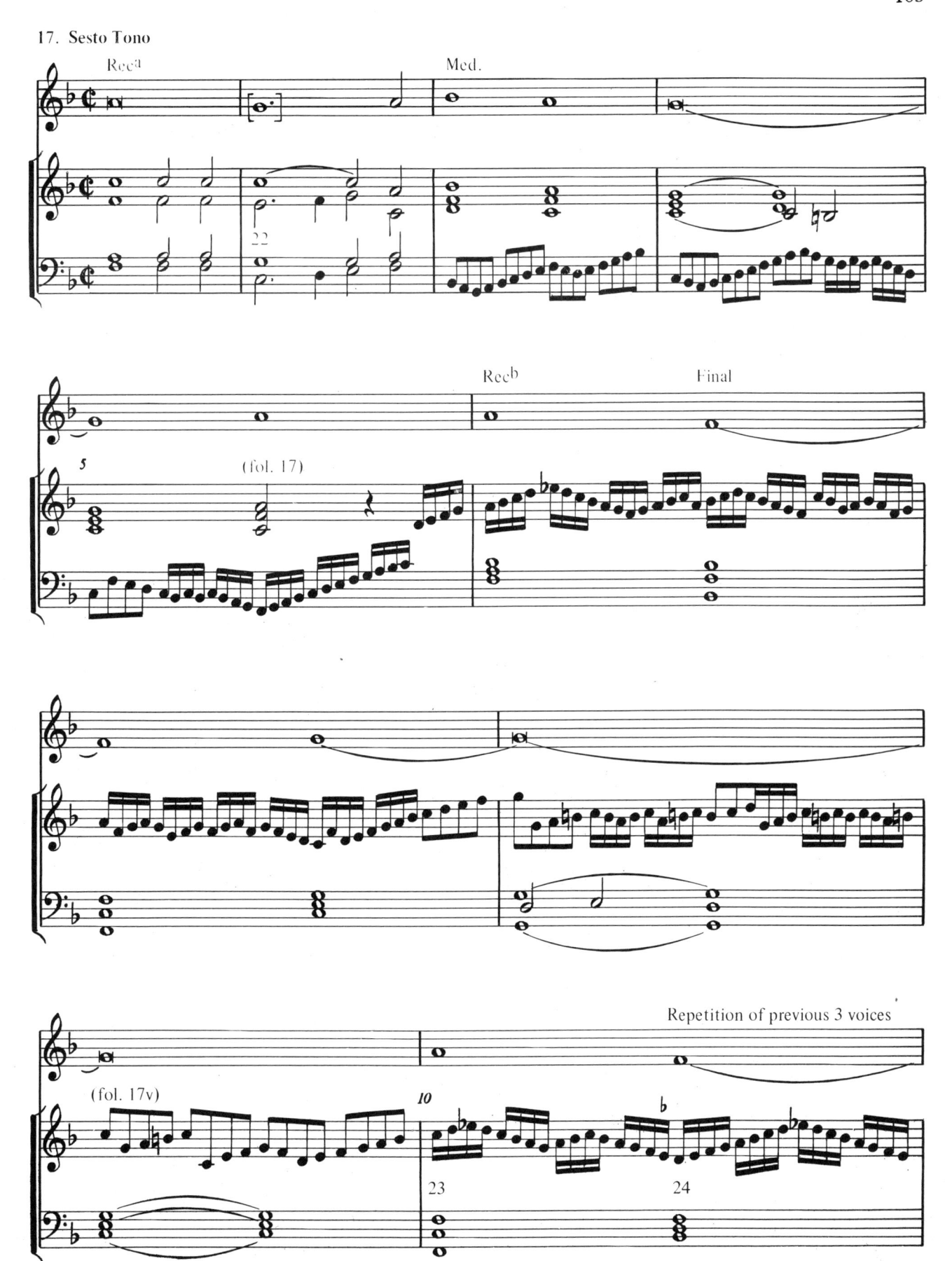

17. Sesto Tono

²² Original: the tenor note g^1 is a minim (half note).

²³ Original: *A-e-a*.

²⁴ Original: *d-f-a*.

106

18. Settimo Tono

107

108

19. Ottauo Tono

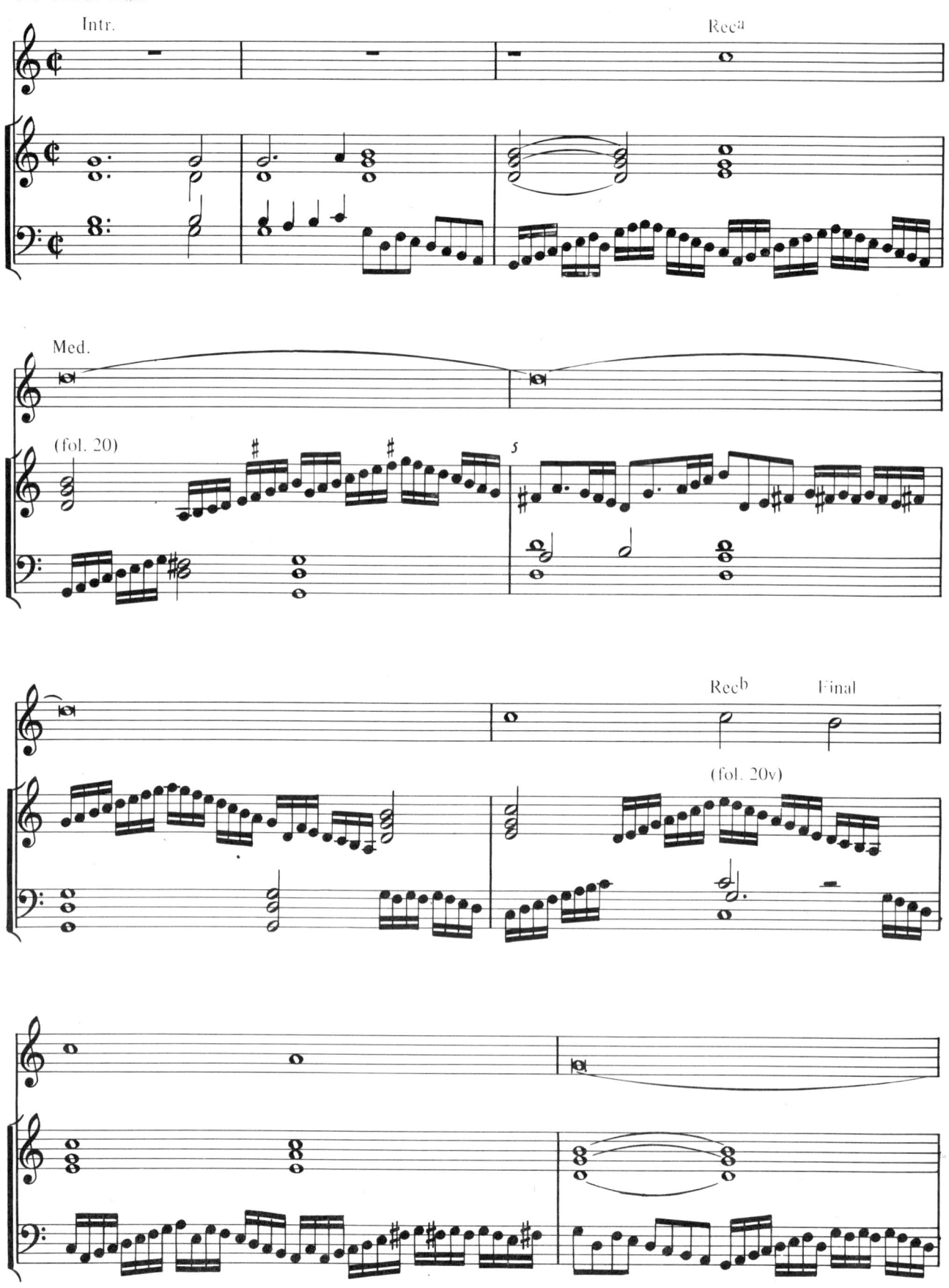

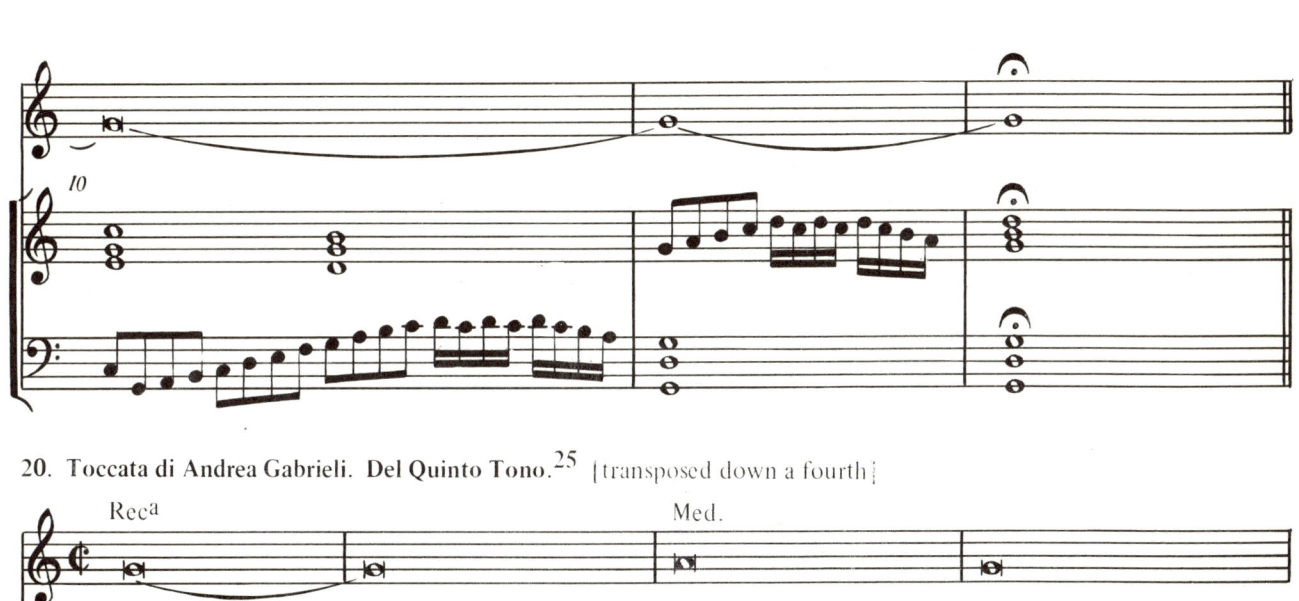

20. Toccata di Andrea Gabrieli. Del Quinto Tono.[25] [transposed down a fourth]

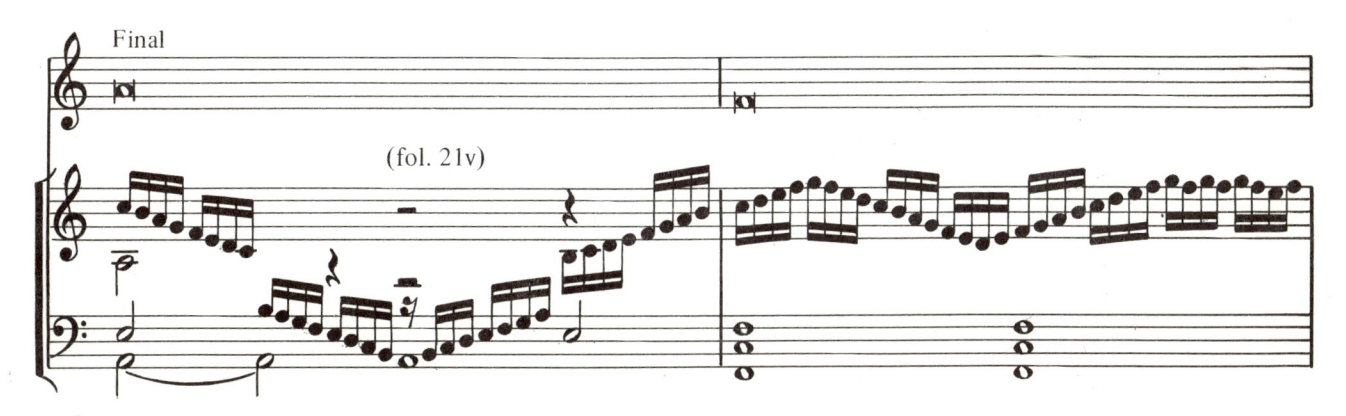

[25] The original is not "Primo tono" as Pidoux asserts (*Andrea Gabrieli*, p. 11).

110

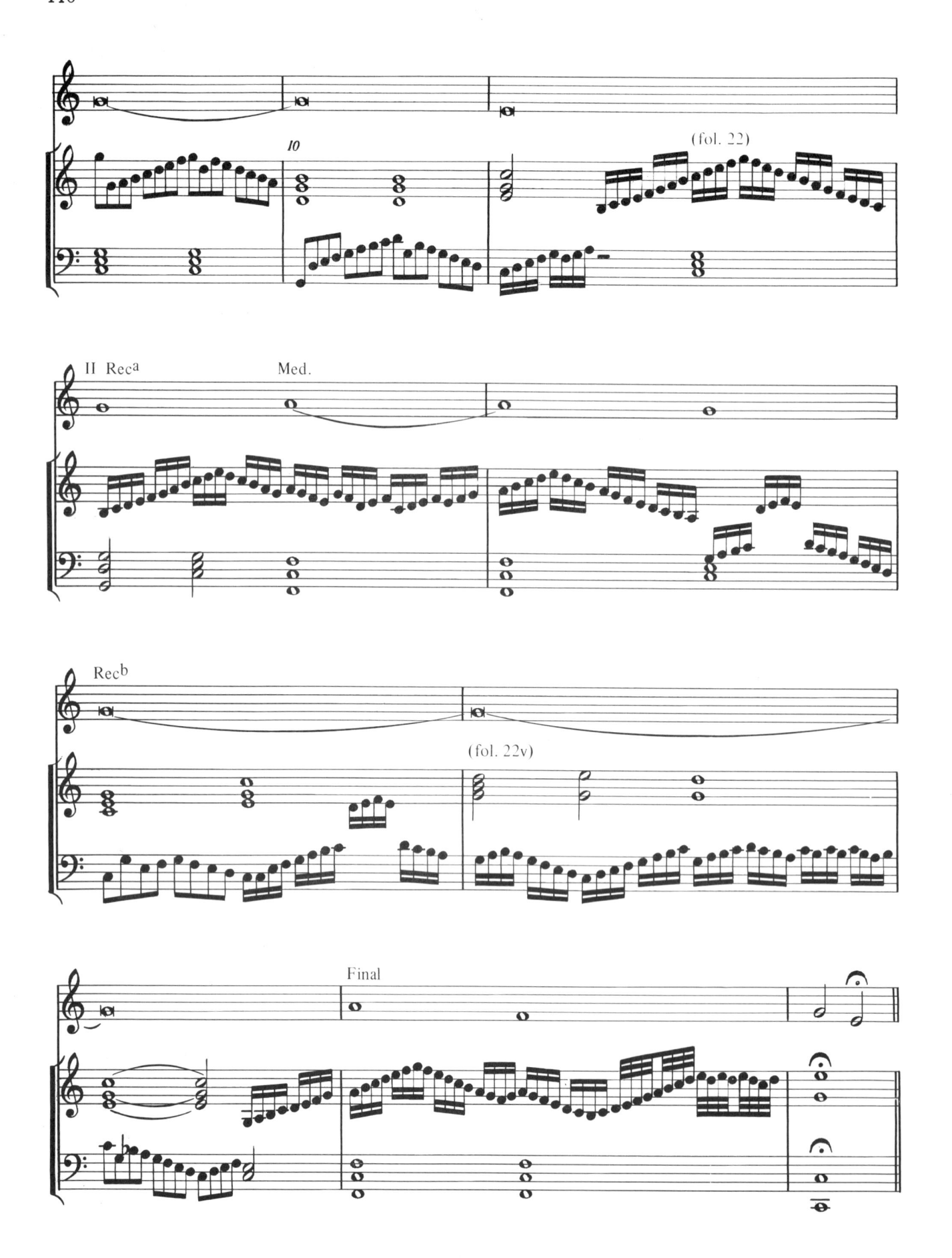

21. Toccata di Andrea Gabrieli. Del Sesto Tono.

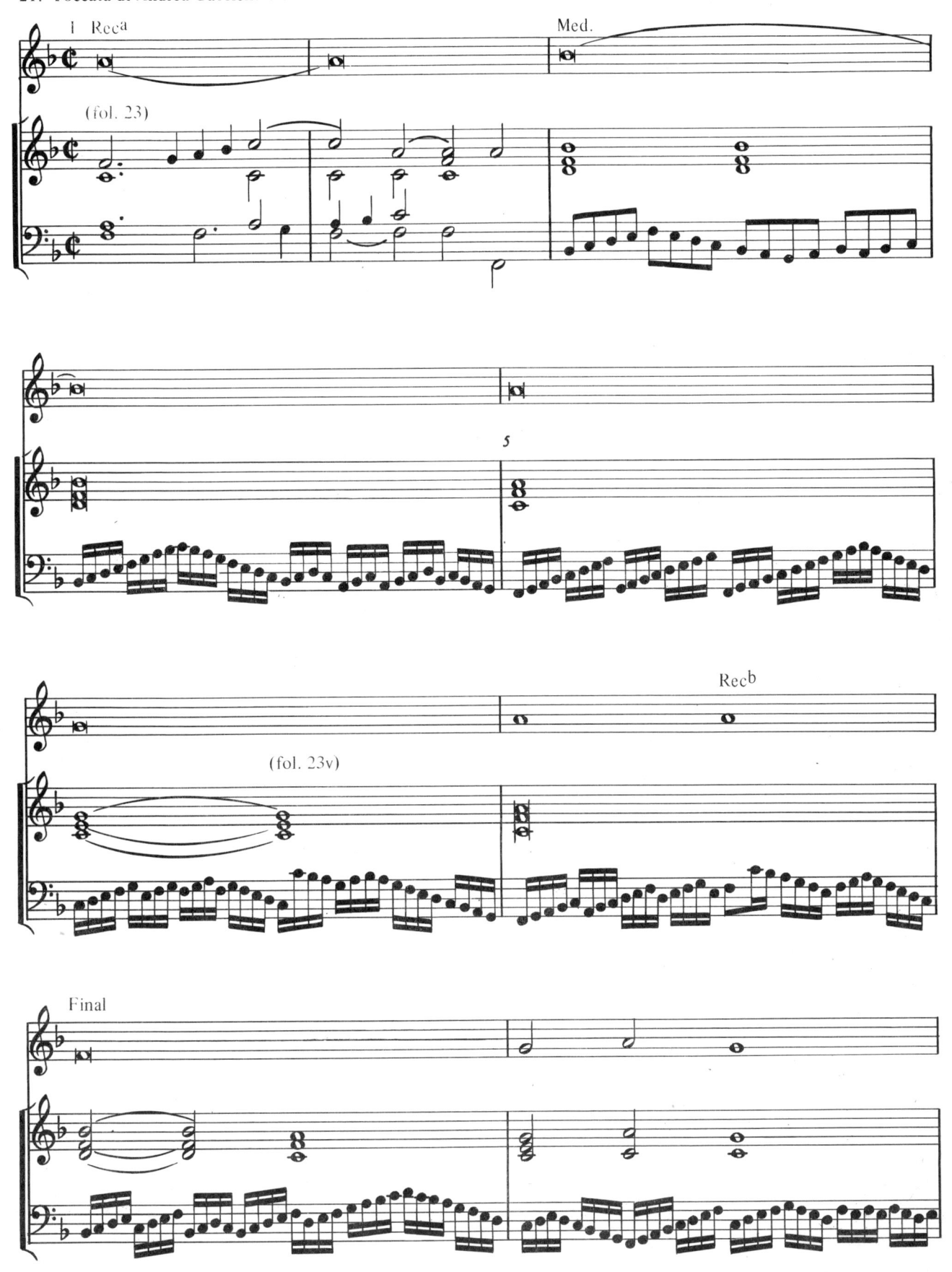

112

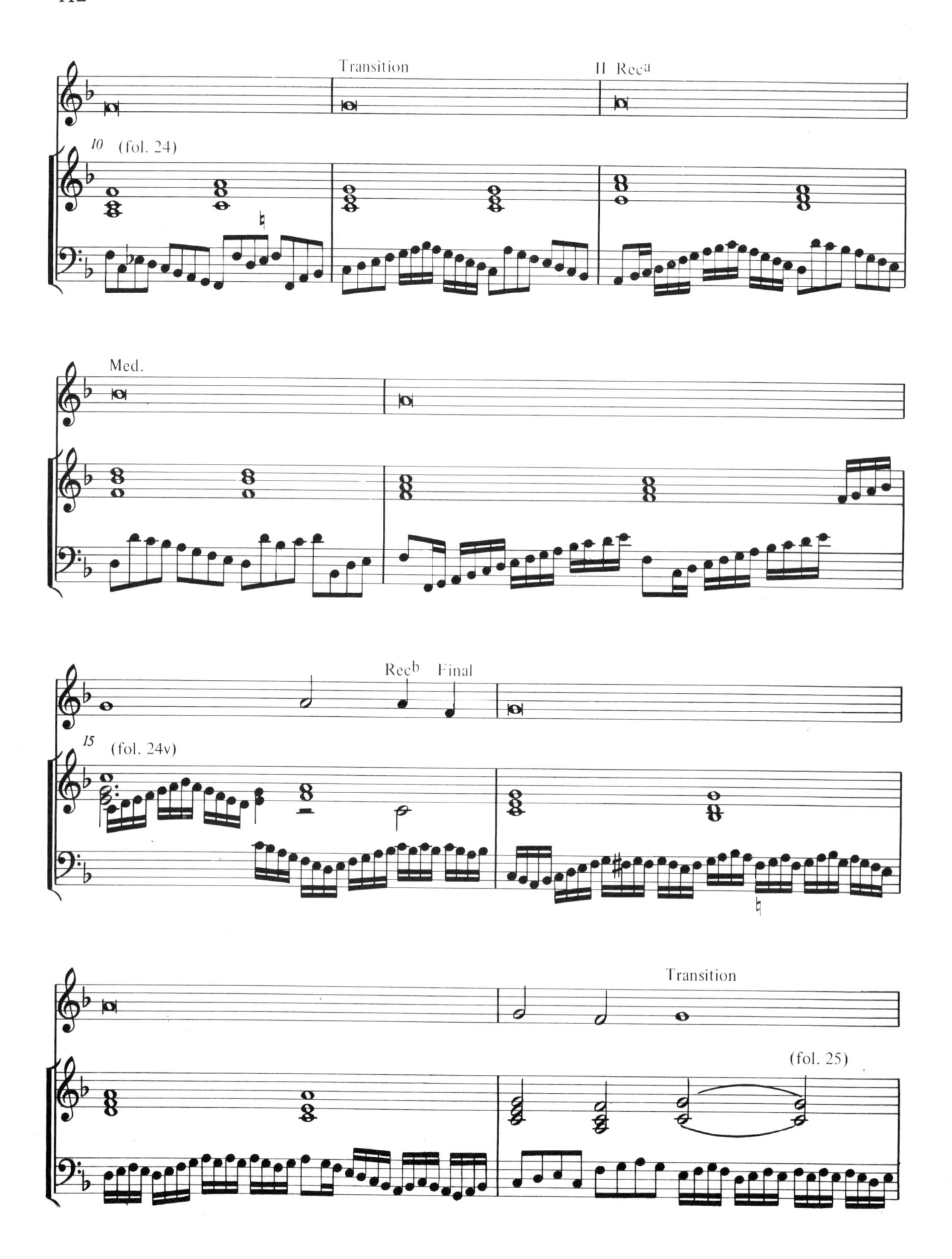

20. Toccata di Andrea Gabrieli. Del Quinto Tono.[25] [transposed down a fourth]

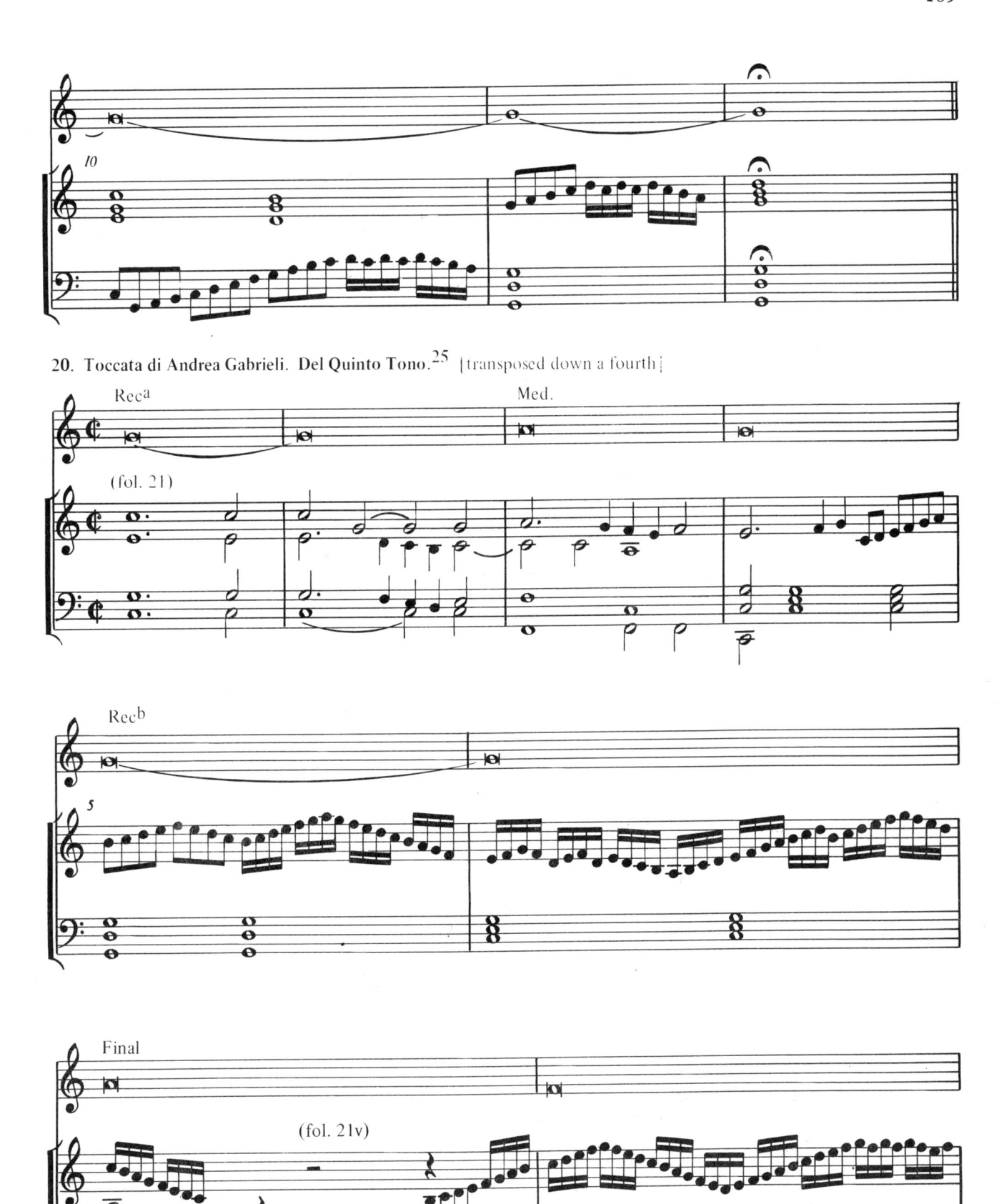

[25] The original is not "Primo tono" as Pidoux asserts (*Andrea Gabrieli*, p. 11).

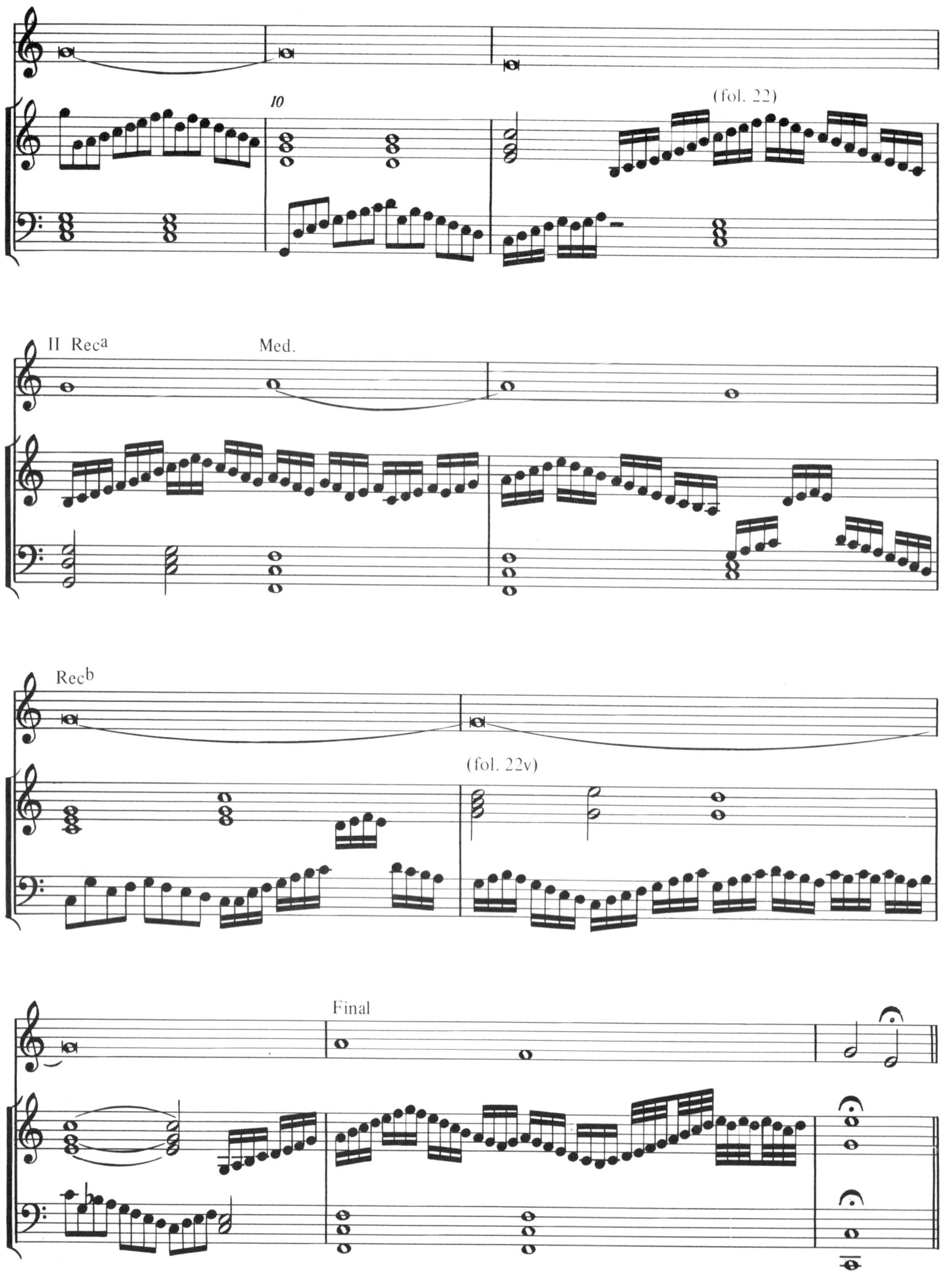
10
(fol. 22)
II Reca
Med.
Recb
(fol. 22v)
Final

21. Toccata di Andrea Gabrieli. Del Sesto Tono.

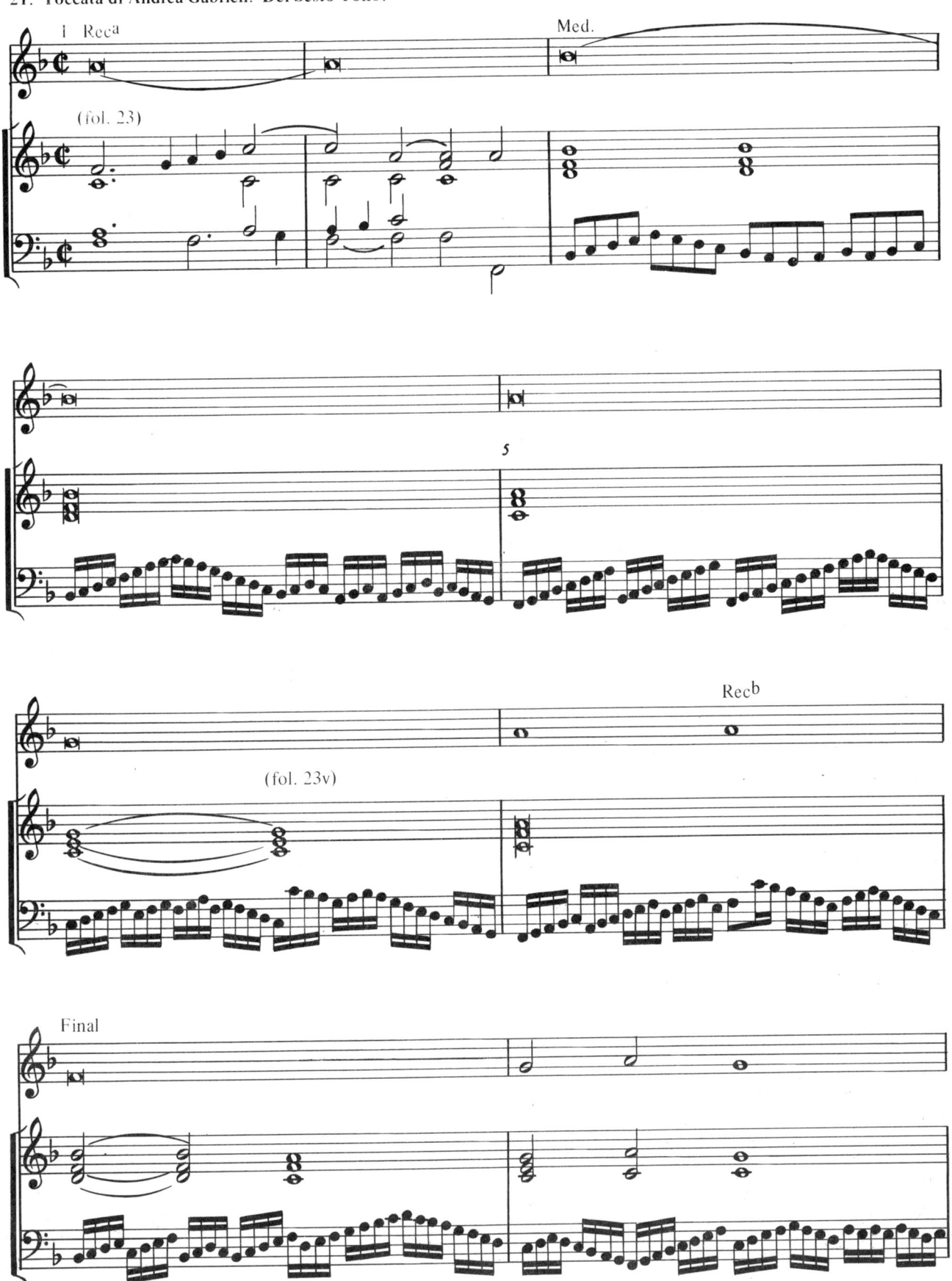

Transition
II Reca
10 (fol. 24)
Med.
Recb Final
15 (fol. 24v)
Transition
(fol. 25)

121

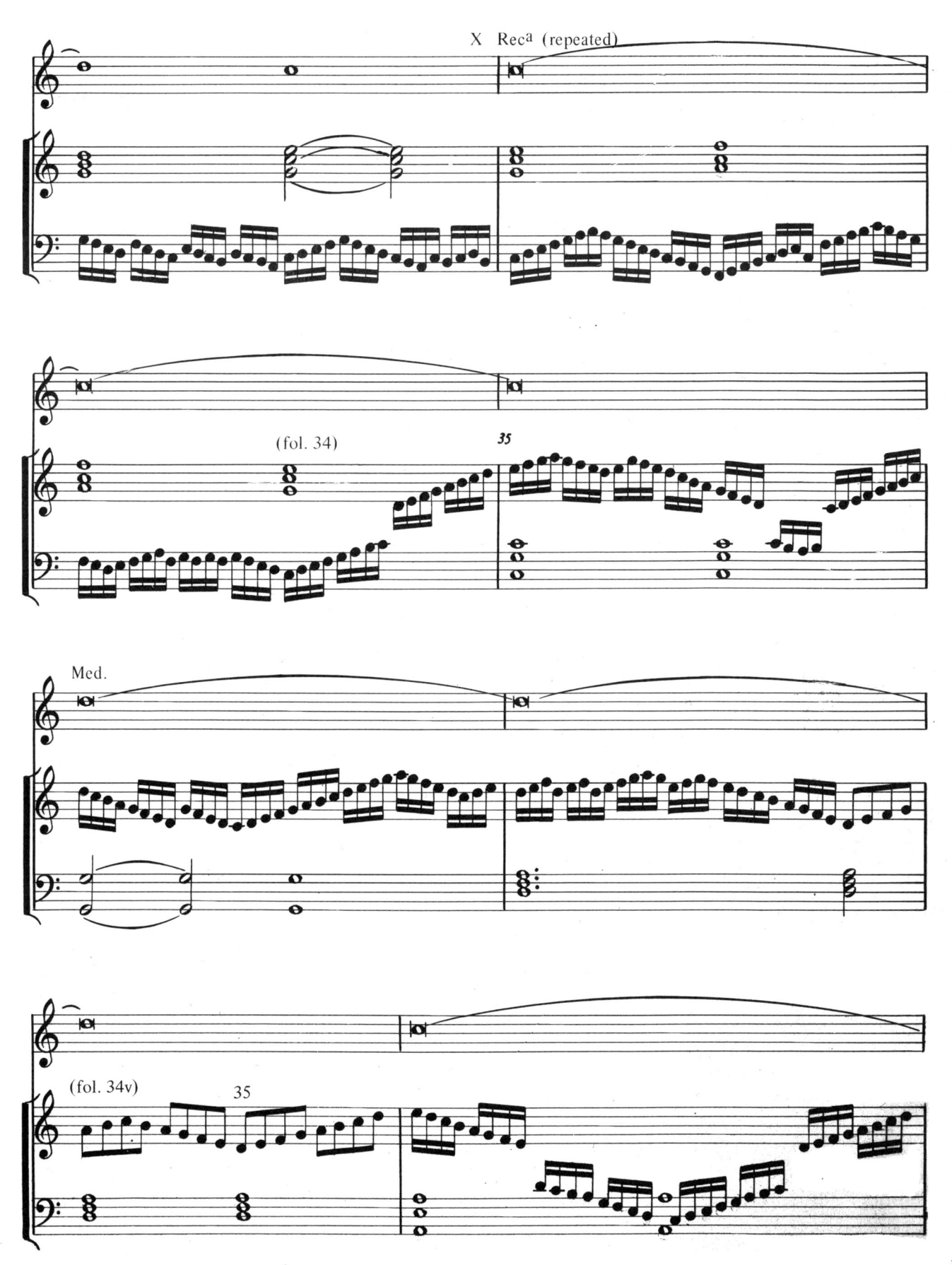

X Rec^a (repeated)

(fol. 34)   35

Med.

(fol. 34v)   35

[35] Original lacks the second chord of this measure.

23. Toccata di Andrea Gabrieli. Del Nono Tono

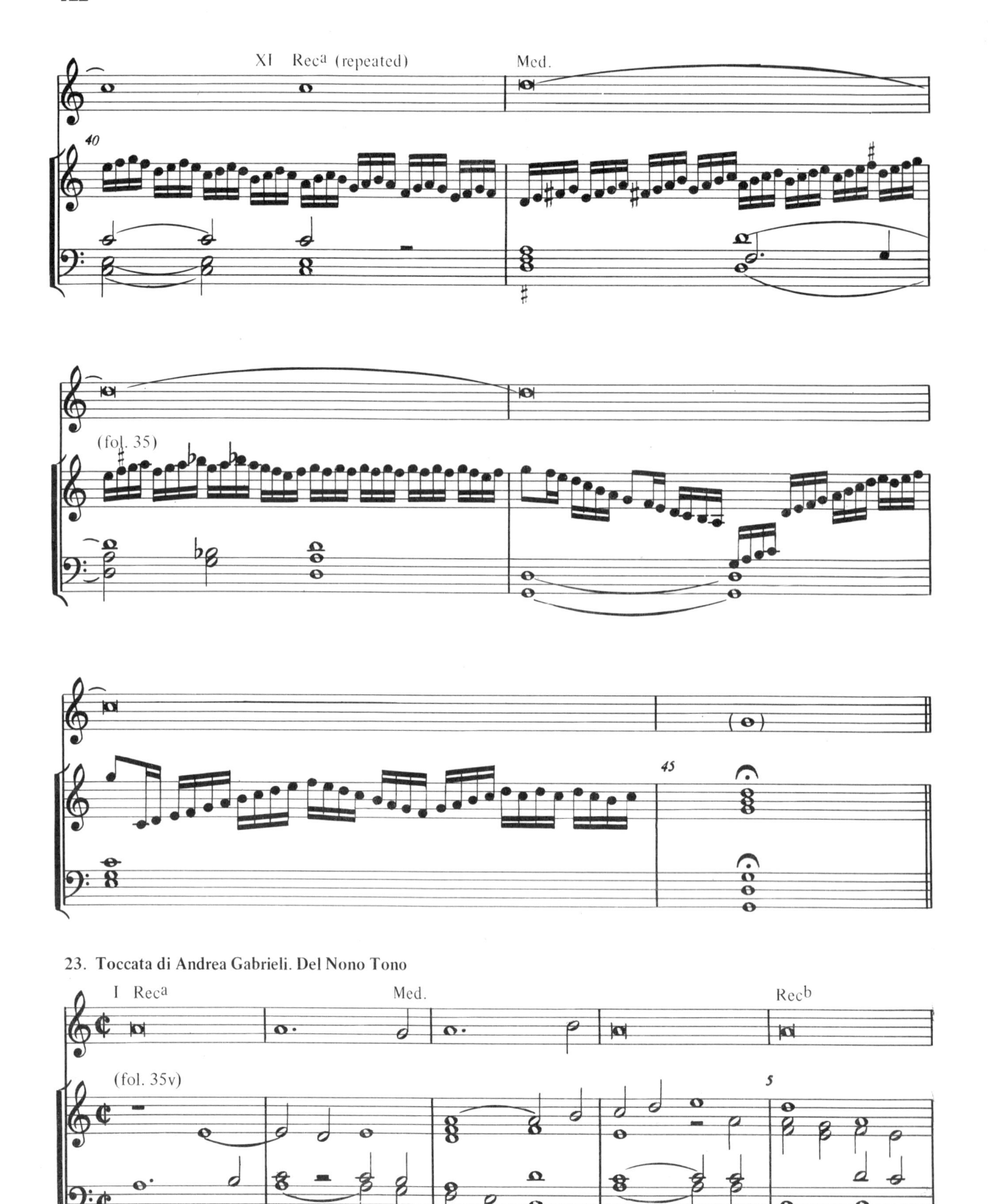

[36] Original has *f* in the bass.

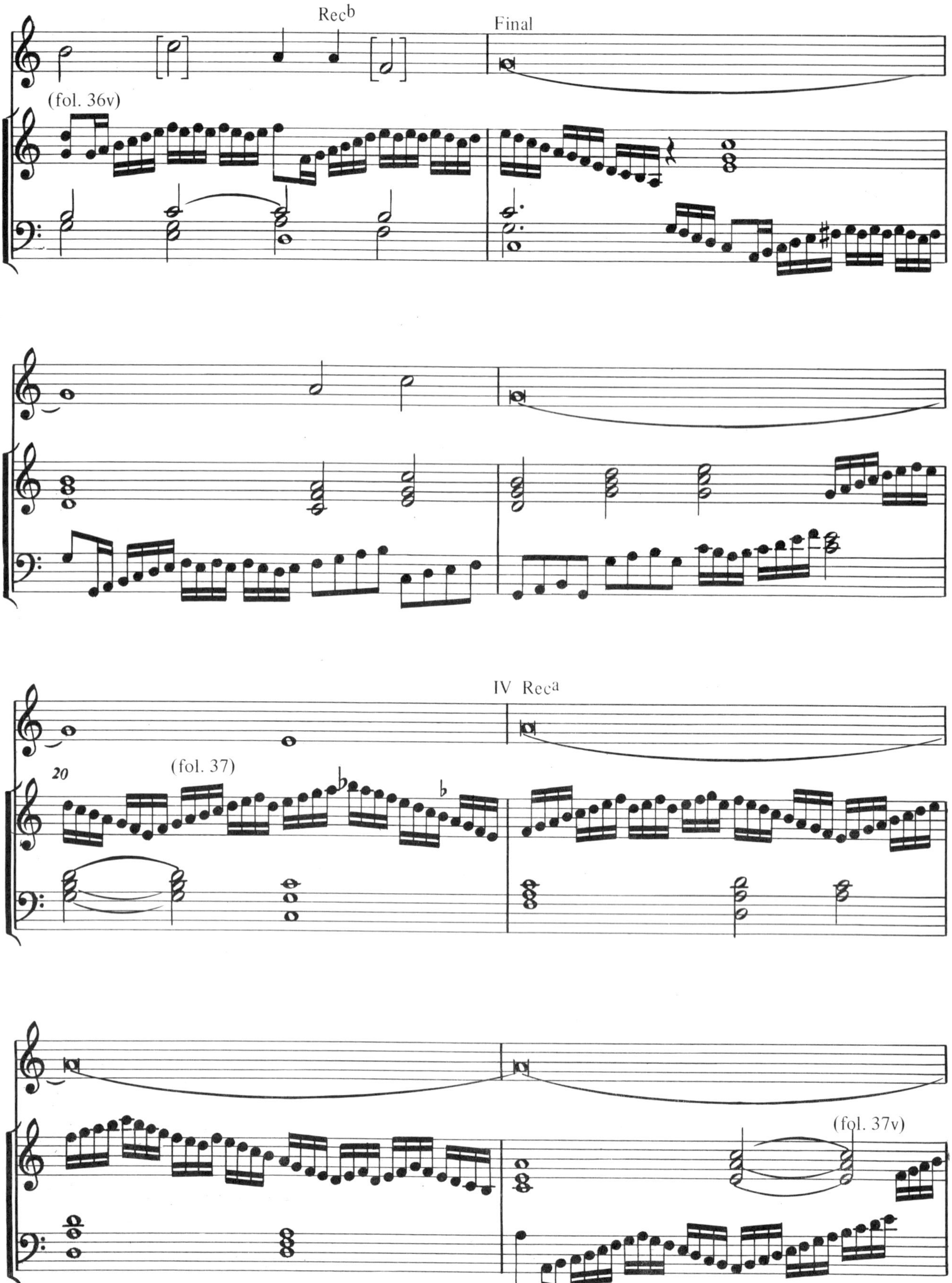
Rec b
Final
(fol. 36v)
IV Rec a
20
(fol. 37)
(fol. 37v)

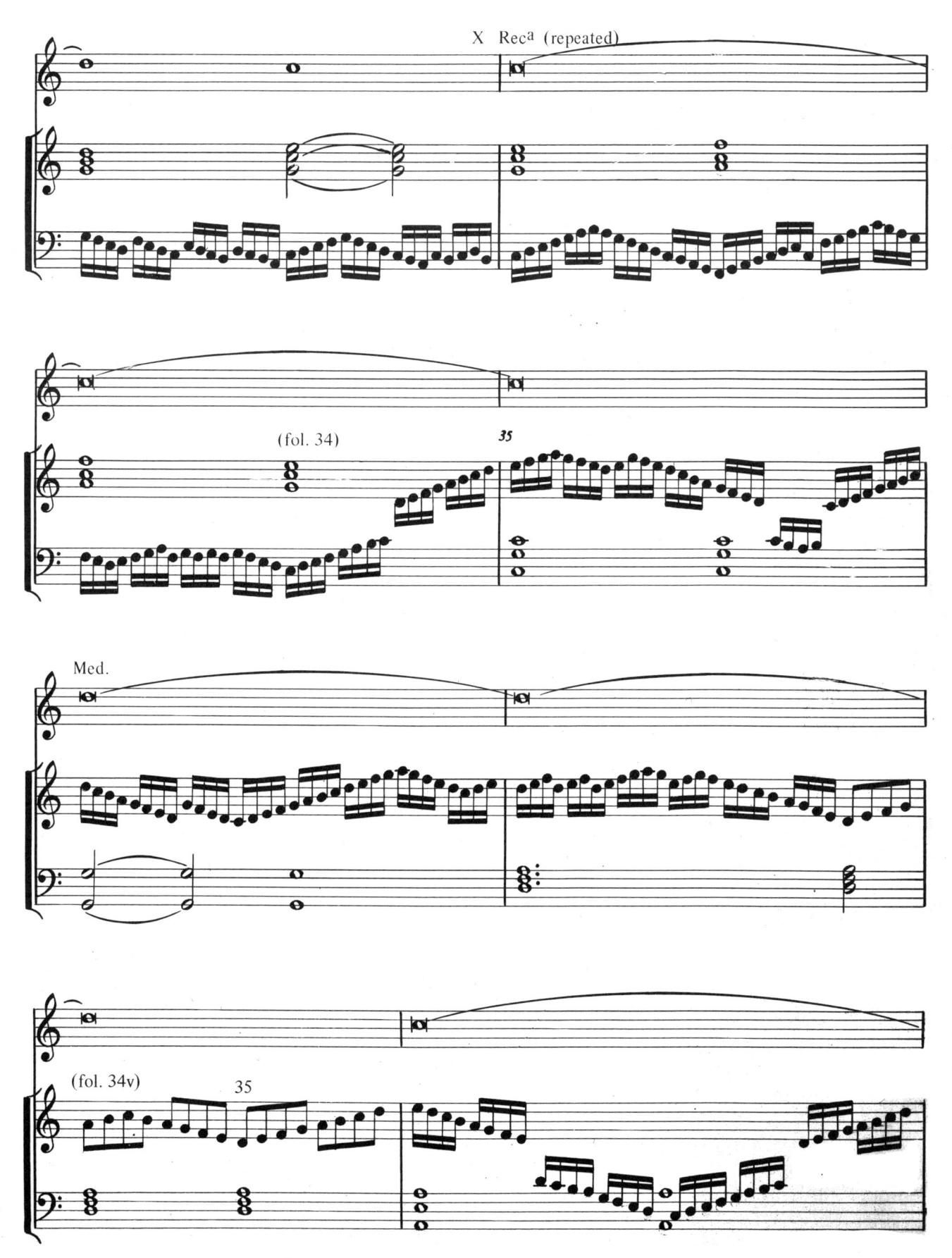

[35] Original lacks the second chord of this measure.

23. Toccata di Andrea Gabrieli. Del Nono Tono

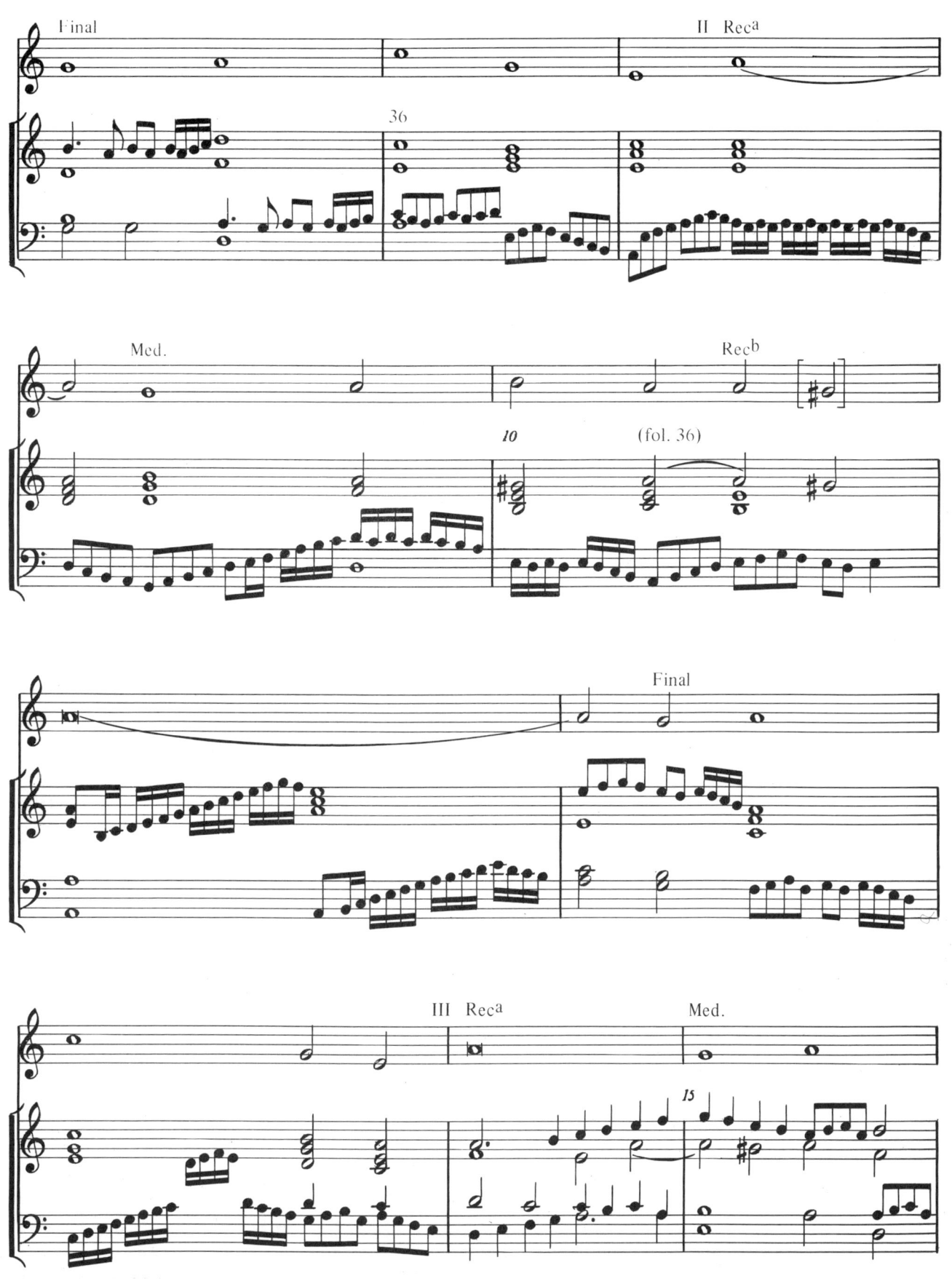

[36] Original has *f* in the bass.

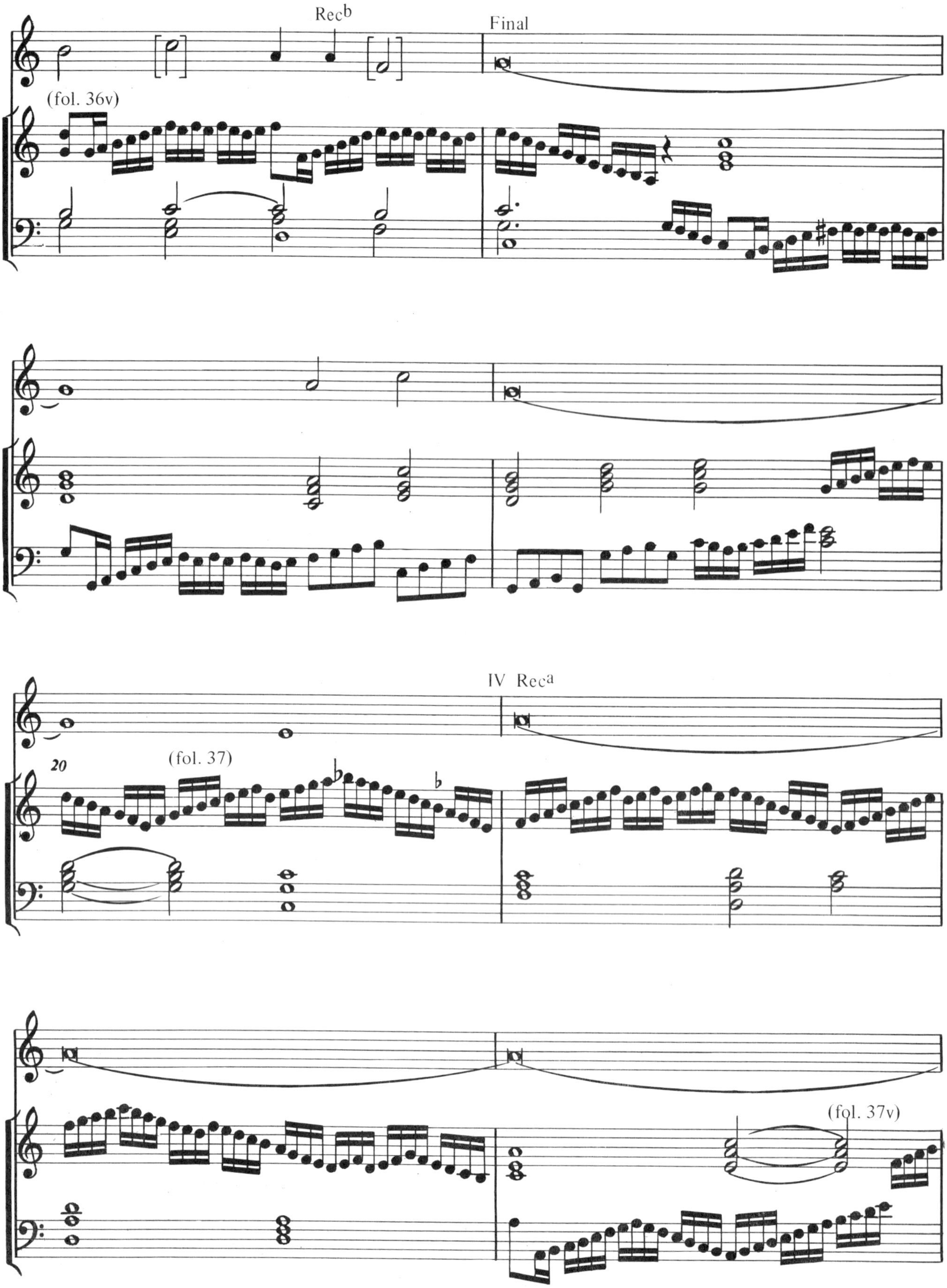
Rec[b]
Final
(fol. 36v)
IV Rec[a]
20
(fol. 37)
(fol. 37v)

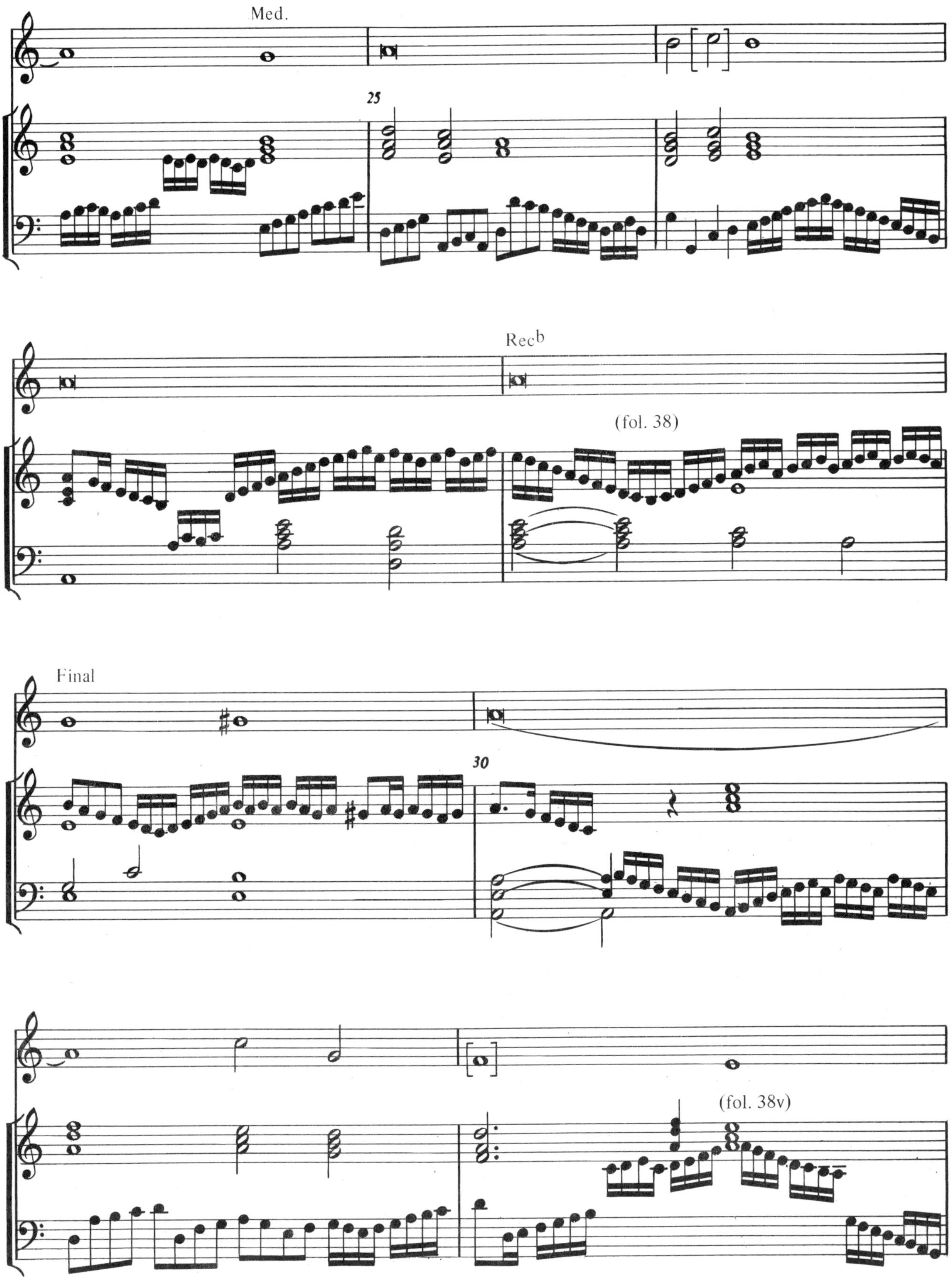
Med.
25
Rec^b
(fol. 38)
Final
30
(fol. 38v)

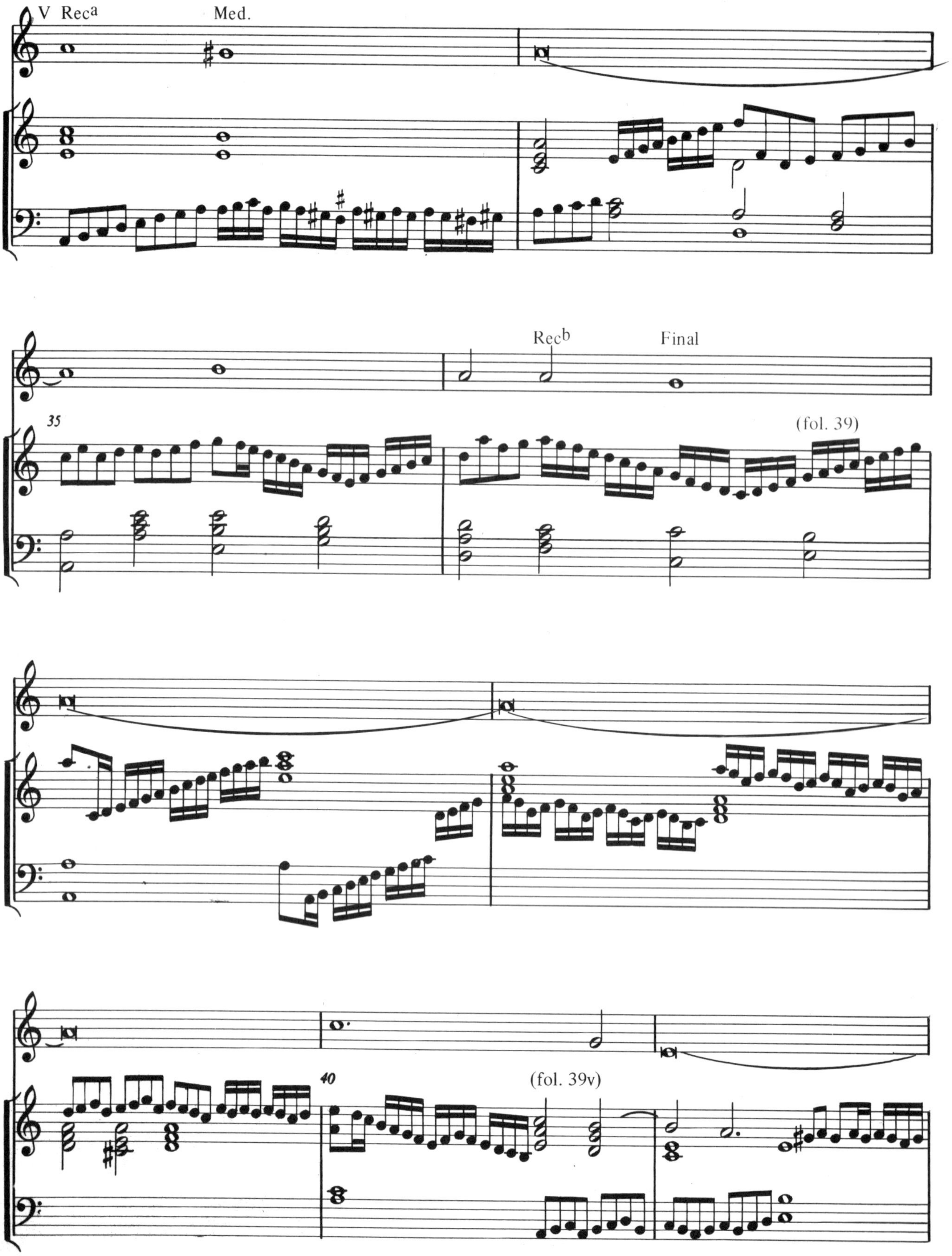
V Reca
Med.
Recb
Final
35
(fol. 39)
40
(fol. 39v)

[37] Original lacks the rest in the bass.

[38] Original treble chord is e^1-a^1-d^2.

[39] Original: last note (b^1) is a fusa (eighth note).

[40] Original: f-b-d^1 for lower notes.

41 Original: g^1-d^2-f^2 in the treble.

BIBLIOGRAPHY

The following list includes only those books, articles, and editions that were of direct use in the writing of this monograph.

Adler, Guido, ed. *Gottlieb Muffat, 72 versetl sammt 12 Toccaten.* "Denkmäler der Tonkunst in Österreich," XXIX/2; Graz, 1960.

Adler, Guido, ed. *Handbuch der Musikgeschichte*, I. Reprint of the second edition: Tutzing, 1961.

Adler, Guido, ed. *Johann Jakob Froberger*. "Denkmäler der Tonkunst in Österreich," X/2; Vienna, 1903.

Adlung, Jacob. *Anleitung zu der musikalischen Gelahrtheit*, 1758. "Documenta Musicologica," IV; Kassel, 1953.

Apel, Willi. *Geschichte der Orgel- und Klaviermusik bis 1700.* Kassel, 1967.

Apel, Willi. *Keyboard Music of the Fourteenth and Fifteenth Centuries.* "Corpus of Early Keyboard Music," 1; American Institute of Musicology, 1963.

Apel, Willi, *Masters of the Keyboard.* Cambridge, 1962.

Attaingnant, Pierre. *Deux livres d'orgue*, 1531. Yvonne Rokseth, ed.; Paris, 1930.

Attaingnant, Pierre. *Treize motets et un prélude pour orgue*, 1531. Yvonne Rokseth, ed.; Paris, 1930.

Benvenuti, Giacomo. *Andrea e Giovanni Gabrieli e la musica strumentale in San Marco.* "Istituzioni e monumenti dell'arte musicale italiana," I; Milan, 1931.

Bonhote, Jean-Marc. *Samuel Mareschal. Selected Works.* "Corpus of Early Keyboard Music," 27; American Institute of Musicology, 1967.

Botstiber, Hugo, ed. *Wiener Klavier- und Orgelwerke aus dem 2. Hälfte des 17. Jahrhundert.* "Denkmäler der Tonkunst in Österreich," XIII/2; Vienna, 1906.

Bovicelli, Giovanni Battista. *Regole Passaggi di musica*, 1594. "Documenta Musicologica," XII; Kassel, 1957.

Bradshaw, Murray. *The History of the Falsobordone from Its Origins to 1750*. Unpublished Ph. D. Dissertation; The University of Chicago, 1969.

Brown, Howard Mayer. *Instrumental Music Printed Before 1600*. Cambridge, 1965.

Bukofzer, Manfred. *Music in the Baroque Era*. New York, 1947.

Caffi, Francesco, *Storia della musica sacra nella già cappella ducale di San Marco in Venezia dal 1318 al 1797*, I. Reprint of edition of 1854; Milan, 1931.

Clercx, Suzanne. "La toccata, principe du style symphonique." *La musique instrumentale de la Renaissance* (1955), 313.

Diruta, Girolamo. *Il Transilvano*, 1593.

Eggebrecht, Hans Heinrich. *Studien zur musikalischen Terminologie*. Wiesbaden 1955.

Engelbrecht, Christiane. "Die Psalmsätze des Jenaer Chorbuches 34." *Kongress Bericht Köln* (1959), 97.

Ferand, Ernst. *Die Improvisation in der Musik*. Zurich, 1938.

Frotscher, Gotthold. *Geschichte des Orgelspiels*. Berlin-Schöneberg, 1935.

Galilei, Vincenzo. *Dialogo della musica antica et della moderna*, 1581. "Monuments of Music and Music Literature in Facsimile," XX; New York, 1967.

Gerlin, Ruggero, ed. *Alessandro Scarlatti Primo e Secondo Libro di Toccate*. "I Classici Musicali Italiana," XIII; Milan, 1943.

Gombosi, Otto. "Zur Frühgeschichte der Folia." *Acta Musicologica*, VIII/3-4 (1936), 119.

Gombosi, Otto. "Zur Vorgeschichte der Tokkata." *Acta Musicologica*, VI/2 (1934), 49.

Guilmant, Alexandre and Pirro, André, eds. *Oevvres d'Orgve de Sebastian Anton Scherer*. "Archives des maîtres de l'orgue des XVIe. XVIIe. XVIIIe. siècles," VIII; Paris, 1907.

Haynes, Maurice Brooks, ed. *Bernardo Pasquini (1637-1710), Collected Works for Keyboard*. "Corpus of Early Keyboard Music," 5/V; American Institute of Musicology, 1967.

Hering, Hans. "Das Tokkatische." *Die Musikforschung*, VII/3 (1954), 277.

Hudson, Barton, ed. *Bernardo Storace (17th c.), Selva di varie compositioni d'intavolatura per cimbalo ed organo* (1644). "Corpus of Early Keyboard Music," 7; American Institute of Musicology, 1965.

Hudson, Barton, ed. *Gregorio Strozzi (early 17th c.-after 1687), Capricci da sonare cembali et organi* (1687). "Corpus of Early Keyboard Music," 11; American Institute of Musicology, 1967.

Kastner, Macario Santiago, ed. *Ascanio Mayone. Secondo Libro di Diversi Capricci Per Sonare.* "Orgue et Liturgie," LXV; Paris, 1965.

Kenton, Egon. *Life and Works of Giovanni Gabrieli.* "Musicological Studies and Documents," 16; American Institute of Musicology, 1967.

Kinkeldey, Otto. *Orgel und Klavier in der Musik des 16. Jahrhunderts.* Leipzig, 1910.

Kraus, Eberhard, ed. *Orgelbuch von St. Ulrich und Afra (Neresheim).* "Cantantibus Organis," 9; Regensburg, 1962.

Lange, S. de, ed. *Apparatus musico-organisticus*, 1690. Leipzig, 1888.

Libera, Sandro Dalla, ed. *Merulo Toccate*, 3 vols. Milan, 1958-59.

Lowinsky, Edward E. "English Organ Music of the Renaissance — I." The Musical Quarterly, XXXIX/3 (1953), 373.

Mahrenholz, Christhard. *Samuel Scheidt sein Leben und sein Werk.* Leipzig, 1924.

Mahrenholz, C. and Harms, G., eds. *Samuel Scheidt Werke*, V. Hamburg, 1937.

Maitland, J. A. Fuller and Squire, W. Barclay, eds. *Fitzwilliam Virginal Book.* Reprint of modern edition of 1899; New York, 1963.

Mattheson, Johann. *Der vollkommene Capellmeister*, 1739. "Documenta Musicologica," V; Kassel, 1954.

Mattheson, Johann. *Kern melodischer Wissenschaft*, 1737.

Merian, Wilhelm. *Der Tanz in den deutschen Tabulaturbüchern.* Leipzig, 1927.

Miller, Hugh M. "Sixteenth-Century Faburden Compositions for

Keyboard." *The Musical Quarterly*, XXVI/1 (1940), 50.

Moser, Hans Joachim, ed. *Johann Gottfried Walther Gesammelte Werke für Orgel*. "Denkmäler deutscher Tonkunst," 26/27; Wiesbaden, 1958.

Praetorius, Michael. *Syntagma Musicum*, III. "Documenta Musicologica," XV; Kassel, 1958.

Reese, Gustave. *Music in the Renaissance*. Revised edition; New York 1959.

Reimann, Margarete, ed. *Die Lüneburger Orgeltablatur KN 208[1]*. "Das Erbe deutscher Musik," 36; Frankfurt, 1957.

Roediger, K. E. *Die geistlichen Musikhandschriften der Universitätsbibliothek Jena, Notenverzeichnis*. Jena, 1935.

Sandberger, Adolf. *Johann Kaspar Kerll*. "Denkmäler der Tonkunst in Bayern," II/2; Leipzig, 1901.

Sartori, Claudio. *Bibliografia della musica strumentale italiana stampata in Italia fino al 1700*. Florence, 1952.

Schrade, Leo. "Ein Beitrag zur Geschichte der Tokkata." *Zeitschrift für Musikwissenschaft*, VIII (1925-1926), 610.

Seiffert, Max, ed. *Gesammelte Werke für Klavier und Orgel von Johann und Johann Philip Krieger sowie Fr. X. A. Murschhauser*. "Denkmäler der Tonkunst in Bayern," XVIII; Leipzig, 1917.

Seiffert, Max, ed. *Jean Adam Reinken, Toccata. Christian Ritter, Sonatina*. "Organum," IV/5; Leipzig, n. d.

Seiffert, Max, ed. *Johann Kuhnau. Zwei Praeludien mit Fugen und eine Toccata*. "Organum," IV/19; Leipzig, n. d.

Seiffert, Max, ed. *Matthias Weckmann. 14 Praeludien, Fugen und Toccaten*. "Organum," IV/3; Leipzig, n. d.

Seiffert, Max, ed. *Sweelinck Werken voor orgel en clavecimbel*. Amsterdam, 1943.

Seiffert, Max. ed. *Tabulatura Nova*, 1624. "Denkmäler deutscher Tonkunst," I; Leipzig, 1892.

Shindle, W. Richard, ed. *Ercole Pasquini (b. ca. 1560), Collected Keyboard Works*. "Corpus of Early Keyboard Music," 12; American Institute of Musicology, 1966.

Tirro, Frank. "The Silent Theme Tradition in Jazz." *The Musical Quarterly*, LIII/3 (1967), 313.

Torchi, Luigi, ed. *Composizioni per Organo o Cembalo*. "L'Arte musicale in Italia," III; Milan, n. d.

Tusler, Robert L. "Master Jan Pieterszoon Sweelinck, Phoenix of Music." *Delta*, II/4 (1959-60), 74.

Tusler, Robert Leon. *The Organ Music of Jan Pieterszoon Sweelinck*. Bilthoven, 1958.

Valentin, Erich. *Die Entwicklung der Tokkata im 17. und 18. Jahrhundert (bis J. S. Bach)*. Munster i. Westf., 1930.

Valentin, Erich. *Die Tokkata*. "Das Musikwerk," XVII; 1958.

Wallner, Bertha. *Das Buxheimer Orgelbuch*. "Das Erbe deutscher Musik," XXXVII-XXXIX; Kassel, 1958-59.

Watelet, Jos., ed. *Charles Guillet, Giovanni (de) Macque, Carol Luython Werken voor Orgel of voor vier speeltuigen*. "Monumenta Musicae Belgicae," IV. Reprint of edition of 1938; Amsterdam, 1968.

Werra, Ernst von, ed. *Hans Leo Hassler Werke*. "Denkmäler der Tonkunst in Bayern," IV/2; Leipzig, 1903.

White, John R., ed. *Johannes of Lublin. Tablature of Keyboard Music*. "Corpus of Early Keyboard Music," 6/I. American Institute of Musicology, 1964.

White, John R., ed. *Michelangelo Rossi (ca. 1600-near end of century), Collected Keyboard Works*. "Corpus of Early Keyboard Music," 15; American Institute of Musicology, 1966.

Wilhelmer, Ambros, ed. *Zwei Orgelstücke aus einer Kärntner Orgeltabulatur des 16. Jahrhunderts*. "Musik Alter Meister," 9; Graz, 1958

Winterfeld, Carl von. *Johannes Gabrieli und sein Zeitalter*, II. Berlin, 1834.

Wolgast, Johannes, ed. *Georg Böhm Sämtliche Werke*, I. Leipzig, 1927.

INDEX

Adlung, Jacob, 43
Annibale; see Padovano
Apel, Willi, 15-16, 50
Apparatus musico-organisticus, 81
Attaingnant, Pierre, 59

Bach, Johann Christoph, 83
Bach, Johann Sebastian, 7-8, 17, 69, 84-86
Bell'Haver, Vincenzo, 14-15, 33, 37
Bertoldo, Sperindio, 14-15, 33, 37
Böhm, Georg, 85
Borrono, Pietro, 61
Bovicelli, Giovanni Battista, 38-39
Bruhns, Nicolaus, 83
Buxheim, 49-50
Buxtehude, Dietrich, 83, 86
Byrd, William, 57-59

Cabezón, Antonio de, 21, 25
Cadence, 20-22, 24, 30, 33, 36, 37-38, 51, 80, 84, 87-88
Caffi, Francesco, 47
Cantus firmus, 15, 20-21, 24, 26-28, 33, 35-36, 40, 45, 51, 53, 55-56, 59-61, 63, 65, 69, 77-78, 81-82, 85-88;
 see also: psalm tone
Casteliono, Giovanni Antonio, 13, 61
Cavaccio, Giovanni, 79
Cazzati, Mauritio, 13
Clercx, Suzanne, 7, 13
Cornet, Pieter, 67

Dalza, Joanambrosio, 13, 60-61
Demantius, Christoph, 42
Dialogo della musica antica et della moderna, 46
Diruta, Girolamo 14, 31, 33, 37, 46-47, 78

Embellishment, 25-26, 38
Erbach, Christian, 72

Faburden, 26
Falsobordone, 19-22, 25, 28, 35-36, 38-41, 43, 45-46, 49, 55, 59, 62-63, 65, 69, 71
Fanfares, 13
Fauxbourdon, 45
Ferand, Ernst, 15-16, 49
Fiori musicali, 77-78
Fischer, Wilhelm, 15-16
Fitzwilliam Virginal Book, 57-59
Frederick the Wise, 54
Frescobaldi, Girolamo, 17, 43, 77-79, 81, 86
Froberger, Johann Jakob, 17, 79-81, 83, 85, 89
Frotscher, Gotthold, 16, 49
Fuenllana, Miguel de, 62-64
Fugue, 30, 43, 71, 82-83, 85

Gabrieli, Andrea, 14-17, 22, 24-28, 30-31, 33, 36-37, 47, 72, 87-89
Gabrieli, Giovanni, 14-15, 22, 24, 27-28, 33, 36, 45, 72-73, 76, 87-89

137

Galilei, Vincenzo, 46
Gardano, 14, 16, 38
Gombosi, Otto, 7, 13, 15, 26
Ground bass, 26, 63
Guami, Gioseffo, 14-15, 33, 46
Guerrero, Francisco, 62-64

Hassler, Hans Leo, 72-75
Hassler, Jacob, 72
Henestrosa, Luis Venegas de, 19-21
Hering, Hans, 7, 16

Ileborgh, Adam, 49
Improvisation, 15-16, 26, 28, 35-36, 42-43, 45, 86
Intonation (introiti), 16-17, 20, 22, 25, 28, 35, 38, 40, 45, 51, 56, 72, 87-88
In te Domine (Scheidt), 70
Isagoge artis musicae, 42
Isoharmony, 36

Jazz, 26

Kenton, Egon, 16
Kerll, Johann Kaspar, 81-82
Kleber, Leonhard, 44, 50-51, 53-55
Kneller, Andreas, 83
Kotter, Hans, 50, 54-56
Krieger, Johann, 84
Kuhnau, Johann, 84

Lasso, Orlando di, 72
Libro de cifra nueva, 20-21
Lowinsky, Edward E., 8, 26
Lublin, Johannes of, 56
Lute, 13, 60-65
Luzzaschi, Luzzasco, 14-15, 33, 40, 46, 78

Macque, Jean de, 76-77
Manuscripts: *Berlin*, MS 40613, 49; *Buxheim* Organ Book, 49-50; *Erlangen*, MS 554, 49; *Hamburg*, MS ND VI 3225, 49; *Klagenfurt*, MS 4/3, 56; *Lüneburg*, MS KN 208[1], 71, 80; *Regensburg*, MS FK 21, 56-57
Mareschal, Samuel, 75-76
Mattheson, Johann, 42-43
Mayone, Ascanio, 76-77
Merulo, Claudio, 14-16, 33, 37-38 40, 46-47, 86
Miller, Hugh M., 26
Modes, 14, 28, 36, 42, 82
Monteverdi, Claudio, 13
Muffat, Georg, 81
Muffat, Gottlieb, 85
Murschhauser, F. X. A., 81-83

Orphenica lyra, 62-64

Pachelbel, Johann, 83-84
Padovano, Annibale, 14-15, 33, 36-37, 41, 46, 72
Pasquini, Bernardo, 84
Pasquini, Ercole, 77
Pedal point, 83-84
Poglietti, Alessandro, 81
Praetorius, Michael, 41-45
Prelude (praeambolon, praämbulum, praeambulum, praeludium), 15-16, 24-25, 41-42, 44, 49-56, 59-60, 63, 65, 71-72, 78, 83, 85
Psalms, 20
Psalm tone, 20-21, 24-26, 28, 30-31, 33, 35-38, 40-41, 43, 45-46, 50-51, 53-56, 59-63, 65, 67, 69, 71, 73, 76-89

Quagliati, Paolo, 14, 15, 33

Recitation, 20-22, 24, 33, 36, 37-38, 55, 61, 84, 87-88
Reese, Gustave, 50
Reincken, Jan Adams, 83
Reutter, Georg, 81
Ricercar, 16, 24, 46-47, 69, 71, 78
Richter, Ferdinand Tobias, 81
Ritter, Christian, 83
Romanini, Antonio, 14, 33
Rossi, Michelangelo, 79

Scarlatti, Alessandro, 84
Scheidemann, Heinrich, 71
Scheidt, Samuel, 69-71, 73
Scherer, Sebastian Anton, 81-82
Schmid, Bernard, 24, 27
Schütz, Heinrich, 73
Schrade, Leo, 7
Severi, Francesco, 25
Sinfonia, 13
Steigleder, Adam, 72
Storace, Bernardo, 84
Strozzi, Gregorio, 84
Symphony, 13
Syntagma musicum, 41

Sweelinck, Jan Pieterszoon, 17, 67-69, 71, 79, 83, 85, 89

Tabulatura nova, 70
Toccata, chromatica ("ligature e durezze"), 13, 77-78
Toccata in modo di trombetto, 13, 76-77
Tonality, 16, 84-85
Torgau, 54
Trabaci, Giovanni Maria, 76, 78
Transilvano, Il, 14, 33, 37, 46-47, 78

Valentin, Erich, 7, 16
Variations, 15, 70
Venice (Venetian), 7-8, 15, 17, 30, 33, 36, 40-41, 43, 45-47, 56, 59-60, 63, 67, 69-72, 75-81, 87, 89
Verset, 21, 25, 81, 85
Vespers, 19, 86
Vollkommene Capellmeister, Der, 42-43
Walther, Johann Gottfried, 85
Weckmann, Matthias, 83

Zipoli, Domenico, 84